Lest We Forget

A Ranger Medic's Story

Leo "Doc" Jenkins

Printed in the United States of America

Second edition, First Printing, 2017
ISBN 978-0-9992937-9-9

www.leoDjenkins.com

Dedication

To the men of the 75th Ranger Regiment, this is for you. My sincerest hope
is that even if we've never met, you can relate to the words which follow.
This was written for you, my brothers, so those outside of our fraternity may
better understand our unique and valuable personalities. Thank you from
the bottom of my heart for all that you've done as my mentors, as my
friends, as my brothers.

"From this day to the ending of the world,
But we in it shall be remembered-
We few, we happy few, we band of brothers;
For he today that sheds his blood with me
Shall be my brother;"
-William Shakespeare

Contents

Introduction

What is life if not the constant pursuit of self-improvement? This pursuit drives us to advance modern medicine and technology. It's what makes men want to join an elite fighting unit. It's why we shoulder the burdens of countless hardships. So it should be no surprise that self-improvement is the reason for this overdue second edition.

When I first wrote *Lest We Forget*, it was almost by accident. I was living with a close friend from 3rd Ranger Battalion in Denver named Iassen Donov. At the time, Iassen was a primary content contributor to a well-known website called SOFREP. In December of 2012, I'd recently parted ways as the co-owner of a successful gym in downtown Denver and was setting out to start another. I was in between college semesters, leaving me with my first dose of free time in years. Iassen asked me if I would write a short story for the site about being a Ranger medic.

I wrote my perspective from a mission known as Operation Simpson, which was divided into multiple parts due to its length. The feedback from each portion of the story was overwhelmingly positive. This encouraged me to write more short stories. Eventually, school started again and my new gym opened. I no longer had the time or energy to write.

Six months later, between summer school sessions, I traveled to an event in Columbus, Georgia, known as Ranger Rendezvous. It was my first time attending the event since leaving the military in late 2006. For several days, we reminisced about all the good times and bad. We told stories absent from my thoughts for years. We laughed and cried and remembered. I recall being overcome by a tragic thought that all of these stories would shrivel and die.

As soon as I returned to Denver, I set out to pen as many of our stories as I possibly could, writing the bulk of what would become *Lest We Forget* in about a week. The intention being to have a sort of journal for our small band of brothers to point to with pride. I wanted men from my company to have a written time capsule to show their grandchildren the time when they were the giants. I wanted something to give my friends experiencing trouble opening up to their parents, children, and wives; to be able to hand over this sort of manual, as if to say, "This is what it was like for me. This is what it was to be a Ranger at war."

My good friends and fellow Rangers, Marty Skovlund jr. and Jack Murphy, each read the short memoir and concluded that it was good, but could be better. I made a few changes, but when classes started in the fall, I once again lacked the time to contribute to the project. Several months later, I experienced a spontaneous, severe bout of vertigo which kept me from moving at all. Sitting on my couch with my head held in place by pillows, I designed a cover from a photo my friend Bryan Wilson sent me from our first deployment together. The men featured on the original cover are all the guys I shared a tent with during my first experience at war; they are all men I admire and respect.

During the three and a half days I was confined to my couch, I created a cover, worked on edits, and read every tutorial I could on how to self-publish a book. In under four days, I taught myself how to format and release a book on Amazon. On December 10th, 2014, *Lest We Forget* became available online in paperback and e-book. What happened next was unexpected, however.

Lest We Forget climbed to the top of the charts on Amazon in its respective category, going toe to toe with widely popular books produced by major publishing companies. Initially I suspected around a hundred people, predominantly my Ranger buddies and my family, would be interested. More copies than that, however, were bought the first day alone. All of a sudden this self-produced book was outselling highly professional works and receiving outstandingly positive reviews. Along with the growing exposure came the inevitable heavy-handed critics. I was ill-prepared for the harshness of some people's response. After all, I wasn't really setting out to write a book for the masses. To date, 263 people have reviewed the first edition on the popular website. While only thirteen of those have been negative, their feedback seems cohesive.

The book is too short, not edited well, and contains far too much vulgarity.

So here I sit now with this feedback, *too short, not well edited, and too vulgar.* Since life is about self-improvement, about being a better version of yourself today than you were yesterday, I present to you the now longer, more detailed, better edited, still vulgar as fuck (sorry you over sensitive fucksticks, this is how Rangers talk and I will be damned if I don't tell the story of these men in their own vernacular) second edition of *Lest We Forget.*

One more thing before you start turning pages—please know that my story is not spectacular. Unlike some of my good friends, I was never Special Operations Medic of the Year. I never received a Medal of Honor, or lost a limb and returned to duty. I never killed thirty-three guys in a single deployment. Those books are out there and worth reading. From my time in uniform to this day, I maintain that I was merely a slightly above average Ranger. There's nothing I have to say that's exceptional among that caliber of man. Perhaps that's what makes this story special.

CHAPTER 1

Cuts Marked in the March of Men

"Victorious warriors win first and then go to war,
while defeated warriors go to war first and then seek to win."
Sun Tzu

The waiting is always worse than the fighting. The cumbersome load of my aid bag pins me to the blistering tarmac. It's securely fastened under my reserve parachute, resting on my full bladder. We're all propped up against our chutes, rifles secured to our sides inside the 1950s-era fabric case, waiting for hours to board the C-130 Hercules four-engine turboprop military transport aircraft. The sweat beads atop the green and black war paint on my face. We receive the order to move, and one by one our Platoon Sergeant helps us to our feet. Like two lines of camouflage emperor penguins, we waddle up the metal ramp into the belly of the plane. Systematically we're counted off, ensuring every member of the team is in the proper place.

In reverse order, we sit down, one shoulder against the inside wall of the already rumbling giant bird. "Pack it in, men!" The jumpmaster yells over the chaotic dissonance of the plane's engines. "Nut to butt!" Meaning one man sits with his back to the cockpit, legs open. The next man nestles in snug, his parachute resting on the lap of the man behind him.

For hours we sit, packed into the fuselage of the plane. No windows, no lights, just the collective heartbeat of over five dozen Army Rangers about to go to work. This is just one plane of dozens en route to the target.

"STAND UP!" the jumpmaster commands.

"Stand up!" we echo back to ensure everyone is awake.

"Hook up!"

"Hook up!" we return.

We repeat each command as loud as we can. The doors are now open, cycling fresh air into our lungs for the first time in hours. My legs are asleep, making the simple act of standing difficult. I'm toward the back of the line, near the cockpit, which means all I have to do is follow the man in front of me, hand off my yellow static line to the jumpmaster, take one hard right turn, and fly.

Typically, the thought of hurling myself into the breeze a thousand feet above the ground with a government issue parachute makes me nervous. I'm not thinking about any of that right now though. All I can think about is the contents of my bladder. I've had to piss since before we boarded. Standing up exacerbates the problem.

We're moving now! Slow at first, a shuffle. Faster, faster toward the door. An uncontrollable momentum grabs me by the chest. Senses are overrun by heat and noise and adrenaline. Every nerve fires at once. The static line leaves my sweating palm and is secured by the man shouting commands. Ninety-degree turn and step.

One one-thousand, two one-thousand, three one-thousand, four one . . . I feel the snap tug of my shoot deploying above me, jerking my body like a rag doll. My legs instantly warm. Like turning off a switch, the anarchy of my senses evaporates into the now brisk night air in an instant. It's so serene. A million stars, close enough to touch. A scene so tranquil, so perfectly paradoxical to the violent jolt which just occurred, and all the chaos to come. I want to grab the moment. I want to remember. I want to . . . *holy shit, I pissed my pants!* The shock of the chute opening proved a little too much for my full bladder. At least it's dark and I won't have to explain myself once on the ground. My aid bag is going to be a little pungent though. I can already see people moving around below me. What a spectacular sight to behold from the ground—the silhouettes of hundreds of Army Rangers descending from the heavens through the pale moon's light, covered in piss and landing on the airfield.

With little visibility and even less control of these old parachutes, accidents in the air are bound to happen. As we plummet to earth, I find myself literally running on top of another Ranger's parachute in an event known as "sky-sharking." I'm not entirely sure the physics behind the reaction, however, two parachutes cannot stay inflated atop one another. I watch in helpless terror as the shoot collapses below my feet, sending my fellow Ranger directly to the earth like a brick. There's nothing I can do. I land softly on a wet patch of grass, quickly collect my parachute, and remove my rifle from the scabbard affixed to my left hip. The now soggy aid bag which sat nestled at my thighs during the long flight is unhooked and on my back in a matter of seconds. As quickly as I hit the ground, I'm moving. I have to link up with the rest of my platoon. The airborne infiltration is just the ride to the office; now it's time to go to work.

En route to the objective rally point, I find a young private kneeling over another man whose parachute is still attached to his motionless body. As I move closer, I hear the eerie sounds of the unconscious Ranger's agonal breathing pattern. His respirations are a mix of gasping and snoring. As I take a knee by his side, I realize this is the poor bastard I sky-sharked. *Fuck.* I instruct the young private to hold the man's head in an effort to keep his neck from moving. I begin my assessment. I can't feel any bones out of place or bleeding. As fast as he must have impacted the ground, he awakens. "What the fuck, Doc?" he yells as his eyelids shoot open.

A tsunami-size wave of relief crashes over me. It's tragic to lose a man, but to have one taken out before the mission even starts, and by the medic no less, that's tough to explain. I make sure he keeps talking to me as I call for additional assistance.

I hate the radio. I never know how to communicate on the damn thing. I spent my youth watching shows like *GI Joe*, which inadvertently taught me bad habits. I have a tendency to say things like, "This comlink lost its frequency," and use terms like "Copy" and "Over" when they're not at all appropriate.

Despite my inept military vernacular, I manage to get the senior company medic to my location within a matter of minutes. I give him the patient's details and inform him I need to rally with my platoon; we've been tasked with assaulting a primary target building. He tells me, "I have control of the patient, Jenkins. Move out to your platoon rally point."

I'm a decent runner; however, running on the uneven terrain alongside the airfield in the dark wearing night-vision goggles and carrying sixty pounds of medical equipment and ammunition slows me down. I'm also not entirely sure where I landed in relation to my platoon rally point, which makes things more difficult. The cold, damp air constricts my lungs as my effort increases. The hot breath escaping from my chest is fogging my single green eyepiece. It's not helping anyway. Without providing the advantage of depth perception, the night vision device is more like a luminous green kaleidoscope, jumping up and down with each impact of my foot onto the ground.

"Doc, we got a man down," I hear as I reach my platoon. The faceless voice continues, "The casualty sustained a gunshot wound," and points to the Ranger lying on his back near a junction box outside of our target building. Seeing a fellow Ranger wounded is never an easy thing to take in. This isn't the first time and it won't be the last. Regardless, my heart still elevates its already increased tempo after the run to get here. My body feels heavy from yet another adrenaline surge.

I feel the cold, wet grass through my pants as my knee hits the ground next to Greg. He's alert and answers all of my questions as I sweep his body for holes. He already has a trauma dressing on the wound. I double check the bandage. A brief moment of pride sweeps over me. The young Ranger I taught to perform immediate tactical combat casualty care did so flawlessly.

I remove an I.V. start kit from my aid bag and go to work. The sticky fluid between my thumb and forefinger means I found the vein. Blood has a much more viscous texture than sweat. With the moon providing almost zero illumination tonight, the subtle tackiness on the fingers of my ungloved hand is the only indicator I've found my target. His stubbled, war-acquainted face doesn't flinch when I perforate his left arm, despite hitting him with the biggest needle in my bag. This one is typically reserved for relieving the thoracic pressure built up by a punctured lung. With the girth of a McDonald's straw, it's appropriately nicknamed "Excalibur" by several of my fellow medics due to its sword-like characteristics. Later, I'll have to explain to my superior medical officer that the near pitch-black environment is the reason why Greg received a lawn dart in his antecubital fossa, but really it's because he's always been kind of a dick to me.

Within a minute, my Platoon Sergeant asks in his calm, yet typically salty tone, "Doc, what's the patient's status?"

My heart rate is back to a normal rhythm. I let him know calmly that the patient is stable. I get a quick 'atta boy' glance from both Greg and Sergeant First Class Strait, who stands over me now, ensuring the well-being of his Ranger.

I'm not sure if it's because I managed to place the massive catheter in his arm under the low light conditions in a matter of seconds, or the fact Greg now realizes the level of autonomy a medic possess when it comes to dishing out and taking away pain on the battlefield. Regardless, he's a lot nicer to me in the future.

We receive the direction to hit the target building a few hundred feet away. I place myself in my platoon sergeant's back pocket as we make our way to the entrance. The sharp pop of a flash bang stings my ears as we flow into the poorly lit building. The pungent slap of gunpowder adheres to the walls of my nostrils. We move fluidly from room to room. In the darkness, gunshots zip off in controlled pairs from my left and right. No movement requires thinking; everything is instinctual. He goes left. I go right. He moves toward a door. I go through. We clear the entire warehouse in a matter of minutes.

Before I know it we're back outside in the crisp winter air. The sweat collecting on my clothes creates an inclement environment. We sit like vigilant statues in the darkness. Minutes seem like hours pulling security on one knee over the building we've just cleared. Joints stiffen like a premonition of the years to come. The silence plays an eerie disparity to the calamity and violence we all just experienced. One beautiful word travels through the radio and into my eardrum, "ENDEX!"

That means we're done. This training mission is over. We will conduct a similar training mission each night this week in an effort to ensure our entire

Battalion is prepared for a mass attack on any airport in the world at a moment's notice. Sleep becomes limited to four hours per night. The conditions simulate the real world as closely as possible. The lessons learned tonight and from the hundreds of other training missions we conduct will become invaluable over the course of my time as a Ranger medic fighting in the Global War on Terrorism.

CHAPTER 2

The Hard Sell

"War is an ugly thing, but not the ugliest of things. The decayed and degraded state of moral and patriotic feeling which thinks that nothing is worth war is much worse. The person who has nothing for which he is willing to fight, nothing which is more important than his own personal safety, is a miserable creature and has no chance of being free unless made and kept so by the exertions of better men than himself."
John Stuart Mill

High school was easy for me from an academic standpoint. I graduated early to attend an EMT course at Glendale Community College. I didn't participate in my graduation ceremony because I was helping pull glass out of a man's arm at Thunderbird Hospital as a part of my final training to become an Emergency Medical Technician. Shortly after graduating EMT, I was accepted into the fire academy at the age of eighteen, making me one of, if not the youngest, member of my class.

I loved the academy; it was my first experience being a part of a paramilitary organization. I enjoyed the physical training and hands-on nature of the course. There seemed to be a deep sense of teamwork and camaraderie which I reveled in. My single father was a captain in a local department and essentially raised me in a fire station. He worked two jobs to keep my two sisters and me in decent living conditions. My father set a shining example of what a parent should be, what a man should be, by taking on the responsibility of both parents and shouldering more than his share of the task. Watching him absorb such a burden to ensure my siblings and I were always taken care of taught me a lesson about responsibility which resonates to this day. I saw all firefighters in a similar way, benevolent and strong, capable of taking care of their own and placing the needs of others before their own.

I woke up early on my nineteenth birthday to go for a short three-mile run before my fire academy class. With nothing else to eat in my bachelor abode, I sat down after my run to a tuna fish sandwich for breakfast and turned on the television. As I ate, I searched for my black leather boots. I looked up at the TV just in time to see the second plane strike the World Trade Center in New York City. I didn't know this instant how this moment would alter my life's trajectory irrevocably.

At first the severity of the event didn't sink in. It was a scene from a movie happening a world away. I knew things were bad from the tone of the news anchor's voice. A person whose job it is every day to tell the world about tragedy is not easily shaken. September 11th, 2001, was different, though; the quiver of his voice echoed over a fractured nation, letting us all know how horrendous an act just occurred.

Despite the depth of the initial reports, there was no immediate impact on what I had to do, so I pressed on. I finished my sandwich and headed off to class. By the time I arrived, the reports of firefighters trapped in the buildings were already coming in. Even as a teenager, I began to absorb the true weight of the situation.

Every man in the room just lost a brother; the collective somber burden fell on each of our shoulders and sunk deep into our souls. I thought back to years earlier when a news report came on TV about a Phoenix firefighter who was trapped in a building and lost his life. Even at a young age I saw how much it impacted my father. The loss of a single fellow firefighter was devastating, whether you were on the same crew or not. Now reports of hundreds being killed flooded the news. We were released for the day to be with our families. The tone was no less melancholy when I arrived at my father's home half an hour later.

It wasn't until months later that the full weight of the day would settle upon me. I was twenty years old, working as a firefighter for a small department in central Arizona. I loved my job; it was all I ever wanted to do since I was six years old and saw my father pull up in front of our house in Glendale riding in the back of a giant, shiny fire engine. I was lucky to have been hired at such a young age.

I had the job I dreamed of since I was playing with Matchbox cars in the sandbox behind my house, but it didn't feel right. Every day I saw video images of Americans my age preparing to go overseas. These teenagers were getting ready to go to a foreign land to protect my American dream. They didn't know my family, but they were preparing to place themselves in harm's way so I could continue my version of prosperity. I stood by everything I loved, yet was unsettled. It's a difficult feeling to put into words, but I guess you could say I felt like a hypocrite. Why should I get to sit back for the next twenty years wrapped in a cape of freedom and security provided to me by the exertions of better men than myself?

The decision to join the military was an easy one by this point. The difficult part was telling my father. I knew how proud he was of me, following in his footsteps. I knew he would be proud of me no matter what, but I still felt as if it was an insult to leave the profession which provided a home my entire life. A part of me felt like I was turning my back on those guys who looked out for me on the job, my brothers.

When it came time to let my father know what I decided, he responded with supportive concern. He always had my back in everything I'd ever done. Everything. I know he didn't want me to go into the military, especially considering our country was going to be fighting a war on two different fronts. He put that aside though and placed me in touch with a former Air Force Special Operations Pararescueman named Bob Vaughn. At the time, I planned on enlisting as a combat medic. Sitting at the dinner table at Peoria Fire Station 192, Bob told me, "There is only one place in the Army for a hard-charging, swinging dick like you. That's the Rangers." He said, "You can be a medic if you want, that's cool, but do it with the Rangers."

I respected Bob a great deal even before I knew the full extent of what a

Pararescuman was. He invited me to his home where he shared pictures and stories from his time in Special Operations. The experience energized me for the challenge ahead. I owe a large part of my success to the advice Bob gave me during that time. Having a former member of Special Operations as a mentor was invaluable. Pieces of advice like, "Be the grey man," would echo through my thoughts throughout my training.

CHAPTER 3

FAR

"Life without experience and sufferings is not life."
Socrates

"**I** can't feel my hands. Why the hell can't we put our hands in our pockets? What is the point of putting pockets in the uniform if it's against the rules to put your hands in them?" I whisper to the man next to me.

"Shut up, man. You wanna get us smoked?" he drills back, his angry breath escaping into the frigid, dark morning in a small cloud of fear and rage.

It's late November 2003, the first day of the infamous Ranger Indoctrination Program, or RIP for short. Even the name suggests that we're all in for a near-death experience. In the last nine months I graduated from Basic Combat Training, Army Combat Medic School, Airborne School, and spent a month in the pre-RIP purgatory to get here.

There are one hundred and fifty of us standing in formation waiting for the inevitable madness to begin. That number is down significantly from the close to five hundred in our RIP-hold group. There are simply too many guys coming out of Airborne school and not enough equipment for them to start a class. Every month the top one hundred and fifty physical agility scores get spots to the next RIP class, the rest roll back into a holding pattern that some

15

say is worse than RIP itself. The PT test is nothing special- it consists of two minutes of max effort push-ups, two minutes of max effort sit-ups, and a two-mile run.

There's no agenda in pre-RIP. While waiting for the next class to start, candidates are tasked out to anyone on post who needs something remedial done. We pull weeds, get smoked, paint curbs, get smoked, move furniture, get smoked, change targets at shooting ranges, get smoked, stand around in formation for hours on end, and then, you guessed it, get smoked. Getting smoked is an interesting occurrence.

The first time it happens it's confusing. I recall living in a holding barracks known as 30th AG, before starting basic training. Some asshole decided to take a nap in the middle of the day. The Drill Sergeant made the entire group do push-ups. As soon as the majority of guys couldn't do push-ups anymore we had to roll to our backs and do flutter kicks until we failed at that, too. This went on for about fifteen minutes or so. The entire time I couldn't help but think, *why the fuck am I getting punished because this asshole is on his neck in the middle of the day?* I learned there are varying degrees of "getting smoked." There's the quick "We got shit to do, but you were being dumb so do twenty-five push-ups and get up" smoking. There's the "I'm trying to teach you a lesson that will help you survive the rigors of combat" smoking. There's the "I know this kid will quit if I make him do air squats until he pukes on himself," smoking. There's the, "Fuck you, I just got my Ranger tab or my promotion so I'm going to mess you up because I've been getting messed up every day for the last two years" smoking. And my personal favorite the "I don't even have a reason, I'm just fucking bored and I outrank you so start doing push-ups" smoking.

These torture sessions include movements that make most CrossFit workouts seem like a trip to day camp. Things like "little man in the woods" and "eight-count body builders" or my personal favorite, the "yes-no-maybe." As bad as getting screamed at while doing hundreds if not thousands of repetitions of various calisthenics is, the worst is being made to stand in one place without moving for hours at a time. The throbbing in your joints after an Ironman pales in comparison to standing motionless on concrete all day.

One Friday while still in RIP-hold, our cadre partially emerged from a window in front of our formation and called for a private. Five guys from the front row ran over immediately. Of course, he didn't ask for five, he asked for one, so we all got smoked. "RECOVER!" the cadre shouted, and we stand up. "You, you, you and you, get the fuck back in formation. YOU! I will let this entire formation leave for the weekend if you can sing a Britney Spears song right now!" He panicked, not wanting the five hundred guys in front of him to think he knows lyrics to a Britney Spears song.

"Three . . . two . . . one. Chance is up, get back in line, asshole! Looks like none of you are going home anytime soon," shouted the cadre. He shut the window and returned to his nice warm office. Thirty minutes later he emerged once again. This time he singled out one guy. "You! Get up here and sing me a Britney song or so help me God I will leave you all out here all fucking night!"

"BABY BABY HOW WAS I SUPPOSED TO KNOW . . ."

"HAHA, help him out, fuckers!" he yelled from the window. The collective voice of five hundred wannabe Army Rangers echoed out the words to the teen pop song. By this point, the Staff Sergeant in the window was laughing uncontrollably and could hardly get the words out, "Get the fuck out of here, all of you!" We scattered like roaches when the lights come on. No one wants to be stuck in this place a minute longer than they have to.

I made the mistake of hanging out in the barracks on my first weekend in Pre-RIP. I spent two days picking up shell casings and setting up targets at a range for a group of guys in Battalion. You want to talk about getting smoked, try being a Pre-RIP student on a weekend detail with a bunch of Rangers. I never made that mistake again. Every following weekend until the start of RIP a couple of friends and I chipped in to get a cheap hotel room just off post. We spent our weekends sleeping as much as possible and writing the Ranger Creed hundreds of times. A lot of guys actually failed the PT test on purpose so they wouldn't have to endure RIP after all of the preliminary torture. The ironic thing is the guys who failed intentionally ended up being there twice as long while being placed with other units.

By the first day of Ranger Indoc, falling into a formation is second nature. You have to make sure you are directly behind the man in front of you and directly between the men to your right and left. Everyone is organized by their last name to make roll call go faster. It has to look pretty or you are going to pay by way of physical abuse. The first morning of RIP, everyone is in place early to ensure our formation is squared away. We stand in the cold, damp Georgia darkness for what feels like hours, waiting for the first day to begin.

My fingers are numb from the cold. Despite standing motionless for so long, I can hear the heartbeats of the men around me pounding out in a collective concern for what's about to happen. We're standing on sacred ground. The walls around us are decorated with the accolades from every major battle the 75th Ranger Regiment has engaged in. Beneath our feet is what is simply known as "the blacktop." This two hundred square meters has absorbed more sweat than the floor of a child labor camp in communist China. This blacktop has taken away more men's dreams than the act of poking a hole in a condom.

We stand facing an old white barracks building with chipping paint and cracked walls. The structure used to house the members of 3rd Ranger Battalion before the new compound was built. It's now home to all of us Ranger wannabes.

The large double doors swing open. As much as we want to look at who's coming out, we know better. From the corner of my eye, I catch a glimpse of him. The man who emerges is a daunting figure I will call Staff Sergeant Runza. He's six feet, two hundred and fifteen pounds of caffeinated hate. It's five o'clock in the morning, but his entire bottom lip is packed to the gills with chewing tobacco. Runza holds a clipboard in his hands with the names of our class roster. He begins his instruction. "I am going to call off your last name. Then you sound off with your first name and middle initial. You got that, shitheads?"

"Roger, Sergeant!" we echo back in collective obedience.

The process goes smoothly until he gets to my good friend, Lewis. Runza calls off, "Lewis!"

"Lewis," he responds.

"Your first name, asshole!"

"Lewis, Sergeant," he shouts again.

Before I can even blink, Runza is up close and personal with Lewis. He looks down at the name tape on Private Lewis's uniform, displaying plainly, 'Lewis.' The entire class can feel how pissed off our new instructor is; the group's collective heart rate elevates. His rage is palpable. He grabs Lewis by the collar, giving him one last chance to follow the instruction. "What is your first name, asshole?" he screams.

"Lewis, Sergeant."

"Your father named you Lewis Lewis?"

"Roger, Sergeant."

"You've got to be kidding me! What kind of asshole names his kid the same thing twice?"

"It's my grandfather's name, Sergeant."

"No fucking way! No Goddamn way! Please tell me you don't have kids Lewis Lewis!"

"Roger, Sergeant, I do."

"So help me God, Lewis Lewis, if you named your poor bastard Lewis I am going to punch you square in the fucking mouth!"

"Negative, Sergeant. I have two girls."

"Even God knew the insanity had to stop! Now get the fuck down!"

Lewis knocks out push-ups as Runza continues through the roll call. This is the first of many encounters with Runza. Later in the day, he tells our class he will take us out into the woods, every one of us, and end our pathetic lives. I believe with all my heart he can do it, I believe he is somehow capable of killing one hundred and fifty men, barehanded. I'd hate to have to face him in battle. We're ultimately on the same side, and I'm terrified of this man.

The first major event following the PT test in RIP is the Combat Water Survival Test (CWST). It isn't terribly difficult. The goal is to make sure you're not afraid of the water. One event involves walking blindfolded off of a ten-foot high dive. The cadre is behind the Soldier guiding them to the end. We're instructed to yell "RANGER" and jump. While waiting in line, I witness one of the poor bastards hesitate at the moment of truth. Runza has a fist full of the back of his BDU top, standing behind him on the high dive.

It's sort of push-pull maneuver he uses. The push forces the kid off the diving board, the pull ensures he isn't going to enter feet first. His mangled attempt at calling out "RANGER" sounds more like "RAMMMFER" as his back impacts the water with the force of a Mack truck hitting a fucking watermelon.

The next two days are filled with constant smoke sessions and a timed five-mile run. It's a mandatory pass-fail event requiring all candidates to complete, in formation, in under forty minutes. At mile three I hear an uneven smacking sound to my right. One unfortunate wannabe Ranger just lost his shoe. He's not falling out though. He runs the remaining two miles half barefoot. When we finish the run, the cadre see the kid standing in formation with one shoe and one very bloody sock. They smoke him for being stupid and not stopping to grab his shoe. He inquires, "But Sergeant, if I left formation to grab my shoe I wouldn't have met the standard and been dropped from the course."

The cadre responds, "Oh yeah, you would have been let go for sure, but you're still a fucking idiot for running two miles like that!"

The biggest crucible in RIP is a three-day field training exercise at Cole Range on Fort Benning. All you really know going into the event is that you will be doing land navigation at some point and an eight-mile road march at the end. Neither of these events are necessarily difficult without the compound stress of being on the move constantly with very little, if any, sleep for the days leading up to them. I learn a lot about myself in these long seventy-two hours. One lesson I still draw from to this day; I'm motivated by seeing other people quit. There's something empowering in the tough moments, those excruciating moments when men who you considered of the hardest and most indomitable will, fall away as you continue to stand. Such moments forge the iron of your resolve. I'm not sure how many people quit that first night—maybe twenty? Maybe thirty? Maybe more.

It's an enticing notion as we do flutter kicks and push-ups in the ankle-deep, freezing puddles that accumulate from the constant downpour of sleet and icy rain. Just quit and you'll be warm. The cadre make the decision much easier for many of the men by standing around a giant campfire cooking hot dogs. They take turns leaving the warmth of their bonfire to come torture us throughout the evening. We're out in an open field and I hear the command, "Hit the woodline!" for the first time.

Everyone runs toward the woods, so I follow along. I don't like being second at anything so I sprint the two hundred-meter round trip to ensure I will be the first one back. Not a good idea. Don't do that. Don't ever be the first guy back. I messed up my mentor's number one rule, *Be the grey man*. I spotlighted myself.

Staff Sergeant Strait asks me calmly, "Where is my favorite stick?"

"Pardon, Sergeant?" I reply.

"You went all the way to the woodline and didn't bring me my favorite stick back?? GO GET MY FAVORITE STICK, ASSHOLE!!"

"Roger, Sergeant!" It's a programmed response by this point; it's the only way I can reply. So as the rest of the men are running back to the circle of pain, I'm taking another lap to the woodline to find homeboy's favorite stick. Can you guess how many times it takes to find his favorite stick? I'll give you a hint . . . not the first fucking trip! Between sprints, Cadre Strait helps me cool down by having me low-crawl through freezing, muddy puddles, breaking the thin layer of ice with my face before advancing.

It sucks. It all sucks, but that's the point. Your legs are filled with concrete and your lungs don't feel like they can expand even one more time. The freezing air penetrates your joints, rendering them crippled. At twenty years old, you get a glimpse into the future; you see what it's going to be like to be eighty. You feel frail and broken. The simple truth is, it's just as miserable for you as it is for every other beaten-down guy out there, so when he quits and you keep going, you know you're mentally stronger than he is. That's something you can't buy, something you can't replace.

This crucible builds a lasting confidence. It's the dividing line between us and them. It's the not-so-subtle nuance of being a Ranger, SEAL, PJ, or any other member of special operations. After stepping through this fire, you know day in and day out you get to go to work with a group of guys who didn't quit when things got tough and that's invaluable, that's why we suffer through this moment.

Just because I survived Cole Range doesn't mean I'm going to be handed a tan beret. There are still two more weeks of events designed to weed candidates out. (Ranger selection is now an eight-week process known as RASP, Ranger Assessment and Selection Program.) Another event that keeps a lot of guys from graduating is the twelve-mile road march. It requires each man to be within arm's reach of the man in front of him. No running allowed.

We step off well before the sun comes up. My inner thighs are near skinless before we even start from all of the previous events. New blisters form on top of old blisters as we push forward into the morning. I watch Runza spear-tackle a couple of guys into the woods for running. By the halfway mark, the white school bus following our formation is already filling up. Fall back more than an arm's length and you have to sit on the bus of shame and watch your friends get one step closer to being in Special Operations.

At the end of the march, one of the cadre stands with a scale in hand. Your pack has to weigh thirty-five pounds, not including the water you're required to carry. Here's the caveat—they don't weigh your bag until AFTER the march. I watch a few guys finish the nasty foot movement but get cleaved off and told to join the group of fall outs because their pack weighs in at 34.5 lbs. A lot of guys who fear this happening load their packs well in excess of the standard. I suppose that's the lesson. *"I will shoulder more than my share of the task, whatever it may be, 100 percent, and then some."*

Later we're required to pass a written test on Ranger history. Our test on Combat Lifesaver (CLS, later adapted to Ranger First Responder, RFR) techniques is conducted hands-on. One man is the lead medic, another is his assistant, and the third is the casualty. I try to game this event by pairing up with two other medics, Jess Fisher and Chris Hartman. I take the lead medic role and it becomes apparent quickly to the cadre I have experience. He makes us rotate, making me the patient. Jess becomes the lead medic now, but our grader recognizes he's a medic as well and makes us switch positions for a third time. Without folly or flaw, Chris effortlessly places the nasopharyngeal airway device while simultaneously verbalizing the reason why. "You're all fucking medics, aren't you?" The unamused Ranger instructor asks.

"Roger, Sergeant," we collectively reply, trying hard not to smile.

"Real fucking cute, assholes. Why don't you go ahead and low-crawl over to the other formation." On one hand, we're being punished for doing our job well, but on the other we know we just passed another event. Each event passed brings us closer to achieving our goal of becoming Rangers. I keep a mental countdown to graduation, the way a nine-year-old does as Christmas draws nearer.

We're on lockdown for the final Sunday. The few dozen remaining members of our RIP class keep busy cleaning items long ago been made spotless, waiting for the next round of torture to begin. As I polish my boots for the third time, I remember that in basic training, if we chose to go to church, they have to release us. I tell Jess about my plan to escape for a few hours by telling the staff duty officer I want to attend Sunday services.

Jess and I met in basic training. We were both assigned squad leader positions in our training platoon. He's a great athlete who played soccer in college before joining the Army. Since he has a degree, he automatically promoted to Specialist, E4. His shaved head hides his otherwise curly, dark hair. I admire his calm demeanor. No matter how bad we get crushed, Jess takes it with a grin.

Unbeknownst to me, another member of our RIP class overheard our conversation about church and asks to tag along. I know if more people find out it won't happen. There's no way they're going to let twenty of us leave. "Keep your mouth shut and we'll take you with us." We head downstairs to ask permission to leave. To our dismay, Staff Sergeant Runza is on staff duty.

He's not in uniform. He's sitting with his feet kicked up on the desk in a tank top and jeans, watching TV, his fingers interlaced behind his head, exposing the abrasive, if not heretical, tattoos on the insides of his biceps.

I muster up as much courage as possible to ask permission to go to religious services. He barely glances at us. "I don't give a fuck."

As we turn to leave, the tag-along does something I can't believe. He stops and asks, "Sergeant, what service should we be going to?"

It feels like the moment you see red and blue lights spinning behind you after running a red light and you know you're fucked! Except this guy isn't going to issue us a ticket, he's going to put our skulls through the brick wall. Runza's attention diverts from the TV for the first time as he leans forward, spits a wad of tobacco into the trashcan and asks, "Do I look like someone who knows when church starts? Do I look like a motherfucker who believes in GOD?"

How do you answer that question? Fuck no he doesn't, but I'm not going to say that to him. It's little comfort that he's only staring at the guy who asked the question. We know we're just as much on the hook simply for being with him. The kid begins to shake a little and replies, "I don't think so, Sergeant." Now, that's the wrong answer. Thinking and being in RIP are two diametrically opposed things. Tell him, no, negative, roger—hell, tell him to go fuck himself, but don't say some dumb shit like, "I don't THINK so." It's passive and indecisive, two attributes that will get you destroyed in this environment.

To be honest, I'm not sure how we get out alive. We ditch him the moment we leave the barracks. The closest church is only a quarter mile away. We have no desire to walk a step farther than necessary. Never, in all my days, did I think I'd attend a full-on, choir-singing, Baptist ceremony. It's like a scene from a movie. We walk in wearing our tattered grey Army PT uniforms, with tan lines around our shaved heads marking where our patrol caps sat even with the marching surface (in accordance with AR 670-1, of course). We're greeted by the sharpest-dressed, singing, clapping group of people I've ever come across. We're so out of place we can't help but laugh at ourselves. It's a much-needed comedic relief before returning to the harsh world of our Special Operations selection process.

We make it through jump training and fast roping, the sleepless nights and the constant physical abuse. We endure the gut-wrenching torture that comes from being told today is "all you can eat day" in the chow hall, following days in the field without a hot meal, only to be given two minutes to consume everything on our plates. After which, the cadre sprint us back to the barracks area at a sub-six-minute-mile pace, causing most of the half-digested spaghetti to end up in the bushes. In one of the final events of RIP, Jess survives scoring the only goal against our cadre during "combat soccer." He pays a terrible price, however. Juking Runza and three other cadre members in the process results in an event known as "seeing the wizard," also commonly referred to as "getting choked the fuck out."

All of that's over now though; we're graduating. We'll be receiving our Ranger scroll and tan beret on a freezing cold December morning. As we recite the two hundred forty-two-word Ranger Creed in unison on graduation, the collective breath of around forty brand new Rangers fills the air like smoke clouds leaving a wild fire. We're about to be the most elite soldiers in the U.S. Army . . .or so we think.

From Left to right; Jess, me, Adam, Chris.
On the day that we graduated RIP.

CHAPTER 4

The Running Free

"Many battles have been fought and won by soldiers nourished on beer, and the king does not believe that coffee-drinking soldiers can be relied upon to endure hardships in case of another war."
Frederick the Great

Rumors float around about a new relaxed grooming standard for the Regiment. Regardless, I stop off at Ranger Joe's to have my ears lowered on the way back from the airport in Atlanta. Four fingers across the top, razor around the sides. Up until this point, even the Army "high and tight" didn't live up to Regimental standards. A fresh cut the day before a new week's duty formation. That's our standard. My hair is looking shaggy by Ranger standards after two weeks on leave back home in Phoenix.

A unique anticipation creates a mosh pit out of my stomach. It's an intense mix of excitement and terror. I didn't sleep much the night before. It's my first time wearing the coveted black Ranger PTs. Those glorious tiny silk shorts, so ingrained in Ranger folklore they have their own slew of nicknames, "Silkies," "Ranger panties," "Catch-me, Fuck-Me's" and, well, you get the idea. The collection of obnoxious, heavy grey shirts screaming "ARMY" on the front are now tucked away in the bottom of a bag in favor of the subtle, sleek black shirt featuring the small-yet-imposing Ranger scroll on the left breast. Even the clothes we work out in lend to our role as quiet professionals.

It's twenty minutes prior to our first formation as Rangers, which means it's five minutes before we have to go stand outside in the spitting-cold, grey Georgia winter morning. If you're not fifteen minutes early, you're late. I'm in a barracks room with my friends, Chris Hartman and Jess Fisher, when a Ranger none of us recognizes pops his head in and says, "No formation, meet in the room next to the aid station in five minutes."

Instinctively, we snap to a position of parade rest, feet shoulder width apart, hands overlaid behind the back, posture upright. Before any of us can utter the customary, *Roger, Sergeant,* he disappears down the hall to the next room to pass the message along.

Including me, Jess, and Chris, I count eight guys. We're supposed to have nine new medics in this group. Jess sees me doing the math in my head and whispers, "Voll told me he's held up in Chicago still. Some bad winter storm." *We're fucked,* I think to myself. Up to this point, if a member of your formation is absent, those present are punished. It isn't logical at all, but that's the Army.

Just as I find my seat, the man who told us to meet here walks through the door. Without hesitation, we all rise to a position of parade rest to show respect. "Good morning, men. I'm Specialist Fabra. I will be your point of contact while you are in hold-over. Looks like we're one short."

"Roger, Specialist," Jess chimes in. "Specialist Voll called me. He said he is stuck in a snowstorm in Chicago."

"Yeah, he let us know."

To my surprise, he doesn't sound pissed, and he doesn't drop us.

"You guys will be responsible for maintaining your high level of physical fitness while you are here as well as improving your medical knowledge prior to SOMC. Does anyone know where our gym is?"

"Roger, Sergeant," I reply enthusiastically, only to recognize after the error slipped from my vocal cords that Fabra is a Specialist, not a Sergeant. Over the past ten months of our training to have someone in charge other than a Sergeant was highly uncommon, so referring to him as such came automatically. The other seven guys in the room look at me with contempt, as I'm sure they all believe my error will soon become their burden. That's how it works in the military; if you fuck up, EVERYONE pays for it. It's a good analogy for combat, and an effective way of weeding out those who cannot effectively work as a team. To my surprise, he doesn't drop any of us. He doesn't scream or yell; he calmly corrects me and moves on to the rest of his short brief.

I didn't know Matt Voll well. We met briefly in basic training, and subsequently went through the same training together, but separated in different platoons. I thought he was signing his own death warrant by not showing up to our first formation in Ranger Regiment; however, I find out Matt is somehow impervious to the disciplinary noose which typically asphyxiates other soldiers. He arrives two days later without consequence. He joins Chris and Jess and I in our small barracks room in a phase of our military career known as "SOCM hold."

Typically, holdover status in the military is the worst place to be; it's a unique purgatory. Since you don't have an official job you get tasked to do all the tedious remedial bullshit no one else will. Instead of a job, we have an open-ended wait ahead of us for our next school. Unlike Army Combat Medic School and Airborne School, there are limited spaces for Rangers in the Special Operations Medic Course (SOMC). We make the most of our time in flux. An early formation followed by self-conducted PT, then organize medical supplies and go back to the gym. More often than not, we're released by 1400 and given long weekends.

Surprisingly, our time at Regiment is actually enjoyable. We take full advantage of the long weekends and travel as much as our budgets will allow. In our group, I'm one of only two guys who owns a vehicle. That means I'm almost always at the center of the debauchery.

(SOMC and SOCM are often used interchangeably. However, SOMC-Special Operations Medic Course is the course itself. SOCM- Special Operations Combat Medic, is what you become upon graduating SOMC.)

I book a hotel, pack my bag, and gas up my new truck in anticipation of our four-day weekend trip. We're released before two in the afternoon. I'm anxious to get on the road to beat rush hour and arrive at our hotel before dark. I wait an hour for the other guys to get their shit together. Immediately upon leaving the heavily guarded Ft. Benning gate, I hear Matt's voice screech out from the back seat, "Pull over, pull over."

"What? Why? We just got on the road."

"You can't have a road trip without booze, now can ya?" Matt states assertively as he gestures toward the dilapidated, off-post liquor store. It's frustrating. I've always followed the rules and having an open container in a moving vehicle is illegal. I wait in the truck with Chris, shaking my head in disagreement. Jess and Matt are both older than Chris and I by several years. They both have degrees and both played college sports. They each have four years of previous fraternity-based, road-trip shenanigan experience.

The pair emerge from the shop with a large bottle of Jack Daniels and a bottle of Coke. Chris is only twenty and bears a striking resemblance to Opie Taylor from *The Andy Griffith Show.* He's a quiet guy, not unlike myself at the time. Our two travel partners for the weekend, however, are anything but. The three of them go through the whiskey like Kobayashi through a plate of hot dogs. Within the hour, I'm forced to stop at another liquor store where another large bottle of whiskey is purchased. Thirty minutes later, Matt and Chris engage in a full-on jiu-jitsu bout in the back seat, flailing about like two developmentally challenged fish out of water. Simultaneously, Jess attempts to defeat the child locks because he wants to hop out of the truck to roll under the moving train we're stopped for. It's a shit-show through and through, and the sun is still high in the Georgia sky.

By the time we reach the Florida line, they're all passed the point of being helpful.

"Two thirty-two. Two thirty-two. Two thirty-two," Jess mumbles for the fifth time.

"Some fucking navigator you are; we've been off of 232 for twenty miles. And damn it, if you throw up in my new truck I will kick you out here at the Florida border." Just as I deliver the warning, the half-digested Arby's roast beef sandwich leaves the warm confines of his stomach and paints the front of his shirt in a not-so-brilliant technicolor.

What a dick. I learn a valuable lesson on my first road trip: don't be the sober guy in a car full of drunks. I manage to find the hotel on my own using an outdated map. I'm not happy when we pull into the parking lot after dark, that new truck smell exchanged for fragrance de back-alley dumpster. Instantly, the sight of the ocean washes away my frustration.

All I know about Panama City is what I've seen on *MTV Spring Break*. After nearly a year of Army training, surrounded by nothing but other guys, we're all anxiously awaiting the flocks of bikini-clad college girls.

In the lobby, we observe a table of senior citizens playing cards. We walk out to the pool expecting to see a wet T-shirt contest and find a ghost town. The beach is equally deserted. We go back inside to check in. In his surly tone, Matt asks the older women behind the desk, "Where the hell are all the women?"

She looks at us with curiosity, then explains, "In the winter, most of the hotel is occupied as a time-share for snowbirds."

Collective disbelief sends our jaws to the floor.

Not sure why all four of us assumed there'd be wet t-shirt contests and body shots going on in January.

"Well . . . SHIT!" Jess slurs in his first coherent sentence in hours.

"We did not think this through," Chris adds, dejected.

We decide to make the most of the situation. It's a silent elevator ride to the fifth floor. We drop our bags in the *decor de geriatric* condo and head out into the early evening to find a spot suitable for four testosterone-charged, young Rangers. I drive up and down the strip. Each blacked-out hotel is more depressing than the last. The best we can do is warm beer and cold chicken wings at Hooters. The high point of the evening is watching Jess react to being denied service due to his lack of sobriety.

The next morning, we wake up late. The stale aroma of whiskey seeps from our pores and permeates the single room our meager paychecks will allow. The four of us engage in an eloquent conversation regarding our next course of action.

"Food."

"Ugh."

"Yeah."

"Uh-huh."

It's unanimous. We drive in circles for forty minutes. All we can find open is a shit-hole Chinese buffet. Before taking his seat, Matt orders a double Jack and Coke, something I've never seen done at 10:00 a.m..

"For breakfast? Really, Matt?"

"Fuck it."

He sucks down three more before we're asked to leave. It's the first time Matt's actions result in my banishment from an establishment. It will not be the last. His technique involves a constant stream of obscenities at a decibel level similar to a fire truck.

We drive around another half hour before spotting a place with a dozen Harleys out front. We agree a group of drunken bikers is our best chance for some proper trouble. We pull in and saunter inside. I've never seen anything like it. It's a bar in the middle of a liquor store. You can order a shot and then turn around and grab a case of beer to go. Why isn't this everywhere?

Matt quickly discovers a drink called "hunch punch." God only knows what's in the concoction. The leather-skinned old biker lady behind the bar makes the mistake of telling us in her raspy voice, "I've never seen anyone drink more than two and be able to walk out the door on their own."

Matt, of course, takes this as a challenge. By his third one he begins taunting some of the bikers. Not wanting to wear out our welcome, or get our teeth knocked in, we decide it's a good time to abscond. In an act of sheer defiance, Matt pounds the remaining contents of his third libation and struts out the door.

We quickly find another bar with promise. On the front of the building the sign reads, *Fog Horn Leg Horn's*. Until now I haven't had more than a couple of beers since I'm responsible for driving. Chris offers to take responsibility for getting us home and I hand him the keys.

Matt gets cozy at the bar and orders another stiff drink, while Chris and I start pumping coins into the pool table. The bartender is a beautiful blonde in her early twenties, tall and fit. Jess turns on his midwestern charm with her immediately. I'm not surprised when she flirts back with him right away. Jess has that thing women find interesting. He's a Kansas boy with a big smile and a genuine interest in what you have to say. He uses his gifts to quickly find out where the locals spend their free time. I miss most of what's said because I'm busy getting my ass kicked at billiards by a twenty-year-old ginger. The conversation must have turned political, because in the middle of the nearly empty bar Matt stands up on his stool and hollers out, "You're a Democrat? FUCK YOU!"

Here's the thing about screaming curse words at a pretty girl in a bar; if you're going to do it, which I don't suggest you do, don't fall off of your bar stool immediately afterward. That will make you look like twice the asshole!

His hard head, adapted from a decade of competitive hockey, is unaffected by the fall. We pick Matt up off the floor, apologizing profusely to everyone in the bar, including the little old lady sitting a few stools down. As her wrinkled hand brings the ultra-slim to her puckered mouth, she rasps, "You might want to get our friend under control." We prop him back on his barstool and get him some water. Matt spits on the floor and the elderly woman continues, "He shouldn't do that."

"Oh yeah, why not?" he slurs back.

"Well, because this is my bar, I own it, and I don't appreciate how you're behaving."

Matt's eyes open widely for the first time in hours. I believe most people's reaction would be something like, *Oh shit, I've been acting like an ass in front of the owner this entire time. Maybe I should shape up.* Not Matt. Matt is a special and unique snowflake. He slides down his bar stool, stumbles over to her, sits down next to granny Clampett in the flesh, and proceeds to hit on her.

"So all this booze behind the bar is yours, huh? That's a lovely top you've got on there." Surprisingly, she seems unfazed. She just smiles and takes another drag. Without warning or provocation, the thunderous clap of Matt falling off his bar stool echoes through the bar for a second time. Flat on his back, a bellowing roar of laughter escapes him as he lies on the soiled carpet.

"He should go," she states plainly.

"Yeah, that's not a bad idea," Chris agrees.

As we walk through the parking lot, Matt unzips and micturates without missing a step, urinating free of the inhibition which typically binds a human of his age. Less than a minute later he attempts to climb into the cab of my truck.

"OH, FUCK NO! Your piss-covered self isn't getting into my new truck! Jess already puked in there; you ride in the back."

"Hey look," Jess says, pointing at the dash when the truck starts. "It's only six thirty."

The effects of the hunch punch drinks begin to take full effect on Matt's system. Jess and I manage to prevent him from jumping off of the fifth-floor balcony a few times before we get to our room. We finally have the opportunity to utilize our Army medic skills and conduct a two-person buddy carry back to the room. Chris opens the hideous aqua-colored door and we take Matt to the bed. We throw him face down onto the mattress. Stiff as a plank, he bounces off and hits the floor with a thud. Fed up with his antics, none of us bother to move him. We walk to the kitchenette area, and that's when we hear it—a shrill cry I come to know as an indicator Matt is past the point of reasoning. It's the first time I hear him yell, "I DO WHAT I WANT!"

Like a zombie on cocaine, he goes from dead on the floor to full sprint in an instant. I have no idea what he's thinking as he bolts, full speed, face first into the closed aqua-colored door. Bouncing like a pinball, he spins slightly, then strikes the back of his head on the bathroom doorframe. One complete, graceless standing three-hundred-and-sixty-degree spin, and *SMACK*, the back of his head cracks on the white tile floor.

"Ohh shit!" Chris yells. "That's a lot of blood!" With no hair to impede the flow, the alcohol-thinned blood pumps from the fresh gash.

A stream of obscenities flows from his mouth as I put pressure on the back of the wound. He flails hard, attempting to fight me off, so I place my knee hard between his shoulder blades. Normally I would feel bad for a guy in this condition, but after the last twenty-four hours with him, my concern at this point is more for my security deposit than the back of his head. I don't want him spraying blood all over the carpet. It takes ten minutes to calm him down before he falls asleep right there on the tile floor.

Before Matt's egregious verbal assault on our beautiful blonde bartender, Jess managed to gather a valuable piece of intel. We now know where the locals will be tonight. The only problem is our good friend just busted the back of his head open and likely has a concussion. Compound his injury with the amount of alcohol he has coursing through his veins, and leaving him alone could mean big trouble. There's only one honorable thing to do—leave Chris with Matt's drunk ass while Jess and I go out to the bar.

In Ranger Battalion, when a shitty task has to be done and everyone is the same rank, we revert to "Time In Battalion" or "TIB." Chris doesn't share our enthusiasm for the plan we hatch, so we explain to him since he's the youngest of the group he has the least "TIL" or "Time In Life."

"Can't believe he went for that," Jess says with a smile as we leave Chris with Matt in the hotel room.

"Uggghhh, what happened?" Matt moans as the sun sneaks in through the blinds and attacks his eyes. "What the . . . why's my head stuck to the sheet?"

Laughter fills the room as Chris flatly states, "Matt, dude, you're an idiot."

We move lethargically, no one wanting to awaken their looming and impending hangover. Matt discovers the paper-clip-size gash on the back of his head and asks again, "Seriously, what the fuck happened? Did one of you ass-clowns hit me with something?"

We all take a near-sadistic level of pleasure in telling him the story. I take a look at the now swollen mess and decide maybe he should get stitches. "Do you know how to do that?" he asks. I lie through my teeth and say yes. Suturing is a skill we will eventually become skilled at, but at this point none of us has attended the Special Operations Medical Course. We each graduated from Army Combat Medic School about six months before, but sutures are not a skill learned and practiced by new combat medics.

We decide to take care of Matt's wounds instead of going to the beach. This is the single responsible decision of the four-day weekend. A stink cloud of day-old stale liquor and bad choices clings to us like a cloud as we enter the CVS drugstore. I'm wearing a dirty grey tank top and am still clearly drunk from the night before. We begin to rummage through the medical supplies aisle. The visibly concerned pharmacist emerges from behind the counter to ask if we need assistance. I ask her in a very calm manner, "Where can we find the at-home suture kits?"

"Excuse me?" she replies, as if this is the first time someone has ever asked such a question. "What on earth do would you need that for?" she continues.

"Hey, Matt. Come here!"

When he emerges from the next aisle over, I spin him around and show the attractive twenty-something brunette in the short white lab coat the extent of his injuries. Her tan skin turns a pale shade of green as she covers her mouth. The site of the swollen, half-crusted, yet still-bleeding scalp must have been a bit more than she bargained for. Without blinking, she shakes her head frantically and says, "We, um, we wouldn't have anything like that here."

"Hmm. Well then, can you tell me where the fishing line and hooks might be?"

"GET OUT! All of you, get out!"

"Okay then."

We stumble back to the parking lot feeling slightly defeated. As we look to our right, a beam of golden light shines down from the heavens on the building next to CVS. The sign reads, *Kwicker Liquor.* We look at each other and have the same thought at the exact same time.

"So you guys wanna just get fucked up?"

"Sounds good!"

"Yup, I'm in."

We roll into the place with the verve of a pack of nine-year-olds entering a Toys R Us. Except for Chris; he's only twenty, so we make him wait in the truck. We emerge victoriously with two thirty racks of cheap liquid gold, Pabst Blue Ribbon. "This should get us through the morning, what do you think Chris?" Jess remarks with a grin.

Well past the demise of those sixty beers and well into the evening, I witness Chris pull off a most impressive move. He somehow dances his way into the center ring of the entire University of Arizona women's water polo team. They're in Florida for a tournament and invite us to watch their next game in two days in Tallahassee. Chris gets one of their phone numbers, and the following morning we make the decision to leave the retirement community to meet up with them after their match.

Since the other three men on this trip are now happily married, I will omit the details of the remainder of the weekend. I will say getting to shave Matt's laced-open head before formation on Monday brought me great pleasure. That wound should've definitely received stitches. Years later, I'm a groomsman at Matt's wedding and listen to him tell the story, flaunting the massive scar with pride, a souvenir of a weekend that would have killed a lesser man.

Panama City is the first long weekend trip of many during our holdover time at Regiment. A month later, we are fortunate enough to be awarded another long weekend. It's mid-February and this time Jess invites us to his home in Kansas. One of the reason I joined the military was to see new places, so I jump at the opportunity to visit a state I've never seen. Once again, Jess, Matt, Chris, and I are set free to have our way with an unsuspecting city.

Jess has a girl back home, and for some reason he thinks it will work out well for everyone if she is our designated driver on Valentine's Day weekend. Of course we don't try to talk him out of it. We're hopeful she has a few morally casual friends who want to join us. The first few nights are status quo. We spend the bulk of our meager month's pay on bar tabs and 2:00 a.m. junk food. Valentine's Day is the final evening we're in town. Someone must have talked some sense into Jess, because he decides to leave us at his friend's house with a couple cases of beer while he takes his girlfriend out to dinner. This would've been a smart move except we're told his friend has a new female roommate. Sadly, she isn't home, so the three of us commence destroying brain cells, twelve ounces at a time.

The two cases of Bud Light are enough to rile us up. Matt and I engage in a fist fight in the living room out of protracted boredom. Chris breaks us up. I go to the bathroom to check to see if my nose is broken. While in the bathroom, I notice a shadow box filled with various sailor knots. It seems to me the bowline is not done correctly. Accordingly, I feel the need to tie everything in the bathroom long enough into the proper bowline. Lucky for me, this girl who I've never met owns several curling irons, hair dryers and other electronic devices with long cords. When I run out of things to tie, I begin rearranging everything not bolted down into a giant pyramid. The project takes at least an hour. By the time I stumble out, Matt and Chris have already passed out on the couches in the living room. I decide my best course of action is to pass out naked in front of the mystery girl's bedroom door in anticipation of her arrival. It doesn't make sense, I know. Don't bother trying to understand the cognitive process of a twenty-one year-old Ranger private with over twenty beers on board.

Unbeknownst to me, blondie came home while I was in the middle of destroying her bathroom, a fact I don't realize until I hear a very loud scream coming from her room while I'm passed out. She runs out in a panic, tripping over me. Matt wandered into her bedroom, mistaking it for the latrine, and commenced relieving himself on the keyboard of her desktop computer. Naturally she screams, "WHAT THE FUCK ARE YOU DOING? WHO ARE YOU?" Matt replies, "Don't worry, I'm Fisher's buddy." It's important to understand, she's never met Jess before. In fact she just moved in last month.

In under a minute she is startled awake by one guy pissing on her Dell computer, trips over another guy naked in the hallway, and flees to her bathroom for refuge to find the entire fucking place tied into bowline knots. Needless to say, we're not invited back. I hear she moved out soon after.

CHAPTER 5

Cuts Marked in the March of Men

"You have power over your mind—not outside events.
Realize this, and you will find strength."
Marcus Aurelius

Every month more young Rangers are added to our group of holdover medics, swelling our number to around three dozen. The problem is, the Regiment only has around a half dozen spots for the coveted Special Operations Medical Course (SOMC) per class, and classes only begin once every three months. This creates a highly competitive backlog. What do you do with dozens of highly motivated, testosterone-elevated alpha males with nothing to do?

The accumulation creates a series of somewhat unprecedented events. The most motivated, physically fit guys from the group without a medic school spot are offered the opportunity to take the Ranger school PT test. The headquarters element of Ranger Regiment maintains more spots than they can fill each month to the leadership development course, Ranger School. Typically Rangers are only offered the opportunity to take the initial physical agility test once they've proven themselves as leadership material in one of the three battalions, after serving one or more combat deployments. For a medic in Battalion, it can be even more difficult to get into Ranger school since the training and deployment schedule requires a medic to be present pretty much all of the time.

Many of the guys in our group jump at the opportunity to earn their Ranger tab before their combat scroll. They know having a tab on day one in Battalion means more respect, and in turn, less hazing. The other option for guys without a SOMC spot is a support role on a combat deployment. A half dozen men from our group are selected to deploy to Afghanistan to assist in aid station and range duties. The deployment means many will receive a "combat scroll" which is a Ranger patch worn on the right sleeve in addition to the one we all have on our left shoulder to signify deployment with the unit.

As a result, some of my close friends manage to secure a combat scroll and Ranger tab prior to even attending SOMC. This may seem like a significant hand up; however, the expectation on these men's ability to perform is now the same as a Ranger medic who has years of experience with a platoon, despite having never spent a day in Battalion. Two months into holdover status, I'm offered a chance to go to Ranger school. I turn it down, knowing the decision will mean I'm at the front of the line for SOMC. To be honest, I don't care that much about Ranger school. I joined the Army with aspirations to become one of the best trained trauma medics in the world and help in the fight overseas. My priority is achieving that end. Three weeks later I receive orders to Ft. Bragg. I pack the entirety of my earthly possessions, toss those three duffle bags in my pickup truck, and head north. With me in this class is Jess Fisher, Chris Hartman, Jake Kopp, Kenny Duever, Eric Ball, and Lewis Lewis.

The long leash which we were permitted to roam on during holdover is cut short and pulled taut immediately upon arrival. We're greeted by a Ranger medic legend known throughout the Regiment for his role in the famed "Black Hawk Down" mission in Mogadishu, Somalia, in 1993. We're told to meet him in the library of the heavily secure SOMC schoolhouse prior to the start of classes.

He enters the room and the six of us stand from the large table in a show of respect. His presence commands it. He grasps a thick walking stick, slightly taller than himself. The object is adorned with tan berets, a dozen at least. He explains to us, "These are the scalps I've taken. These are the Rangers I've removed from this course and in turn removed their privilege of wearing this beret. I have another stick in my office covered with black berets." The message is simple and the visual tool is effective. *Fucking off will not be tolerated here.* The man standing before us, providing our introduction to the course, is the reason most of us are here. He's who we want to be. The salty, experienced warrior who's been tested by the tribulations of combat and proven his mettle. I set my goal in this moment to improve upon his legacy, to carry the heavy torch of the Ranger medic tradition.

Day one of classes has an equally profound impact. We're issued our six-month course load. The stack of books is nearly as tall as I am. Ninety-six college credit hours in half a year. That's the daunting challenge laid out before us. We're responsible for learning anatomy, physiology, pathology, kinesiology, pharmacology, and every other "ology" there is.

"Men, this course is going to be like drinking from a fire hose," the burly, six-foot, senior Special Forces medic instructor professes from the front of the classroom, green beret and spit cup on the corner of his desk. I'm in the second row. To my left is another green beret. It belongs to a sergeant who's reclassing from weapons sergeant to medic. A couple of seats to my right are three Navy SEALs. My head is spinning attempting to take it all in. Every man in this room has completed an exceptionally arduous selection to be here. It's an eclectic mix of badasses.

The majority of our class is comprised of guys in the Special Forces Qualification Course, or "Q-course" for short. They've passed Special Forces selection and are en route to earning their Green Beret. If they successfully pass this course, they'll still have to complete several other phases of training before receiving their Special Forces tab and Green Beret. There are half a dozen SEALs who just endured six months of BUDs, and a handful of Marine Recon Corpsman who recently passed Recon selection. There's also a couple of members of an Army Civil Affairs unit and two staff sergeants from the Air Force, one of whom is female. To my knowledge, she's the first female to be admitted to this course. Additionally, there are a couple of members of Special Forces units from two different countries.

The attrition rate for SOMC is known to be one of the highest of any school in the military. The first three months of the course focuses heavily on didactics. The amount of information we're responsible for learning is incredible. It becomes routine to have upwards of three or four tests on the same day.

The days blur together. Early morning formation, an hour of physical training, forty minutes to clean up and get breakfast, then off to class. Eight hours of PowerPoint and lecture, then back to the small two-person barracks room to study for two more hours during the "medical fundamental" portion of the course. Jess is my roommate once again and is having no trouble with this portion of the school. He already has a bachelor's degree in biology, so for him this is little more than review. At night, he watches old episodes of *Buffy the Vampire Slayer* on our second-hand, 19-inch TV, while I attempt to cram the location and function of the twelve cranial nerves into my already stuffed brain. Cadaver labs and cellular biology permeate my thoughts until my dreams consist of little more than semi-permeable membranes and the sodium-potassium pump. We lose several members from our class through the first phase.

One of the final events of medical fundamentals is a procedure known as the "D.R.E.," or digital rectal exam. That's a fancy way of saying we've got to practice checking prostates on our close friends in front of the rest of the class. I partner with my Ranger buddy Jake because he's skinny and has little fingers. It's a sober day in the schoolhouse. Guys are nervous about this event because I imagine most of them have never received a finger in their ass before. I say most because, well, like I said before, the school has several Navy guys in attendance.

Half of the class stands in a row, shoulder-to-shoulder, and drops their BDU bottoms. It's important to look straight forward so as to not make eye contact with the man to your left and right. Apprehensively we place our hands on the table in front. The goal of the person performing the procedure is to palpate, or feel, the prostate. I discover quickly my friend Jake, despite all his strengths, sucks at finding a prostate. His skinny little finger is in my ass for what feels like the first half of a Monday morning after a weekend bender. When I look up, I notice everyone else is finished and he is still searching. I yell out to him, "Are you fucking kidding me right now? Hurry the fuck up!"

Jake just laughs. "I can't find it."

"Well then pretend you did." I whisper through clenched teeth. The entire class has a laugh at the expense of my now dilated anus. I'd get my revenge later, but for right now all I can do is limp to the bathroom, curl up in the fetal position, and try not to cry.

Phase two is "Trauma." However, before we get to the hands-on portion, there are three more written tests. These are the most extensive of the course. I go into them overly confident and come close to failing the first two. Below an 80 percent on two consecutive tests during this course results in academic probation. Imagine after school detention for a group of Special Ops medics.

Luckily for me, the Ranger medic legend liaison recently retired and his replacement has yet to arrive to the school house. As a result, many of the Ranger privates, including me, begin to lose a little of their hardline discipline. I haven't gone to the barber in a month. I'm looking and acting more and more like my SEAL counterparts.

I'm in academic probation with one of those SEALs named Chris. He's younger than me by a few months and seems to always be testing his boundaries. Chris is a country boy with an affinity for whiskey and women. We get along like old friends. He's what I always expected a SEAL to be, tall and strong, confident with a hint of eccentric. We work together and both get A's on the third and final written test of the section.

The academic portion wipes out nearly half of our class. If they're deemed to be "trainable," they're given the option to recycle and have the opportunity to start again from the beginning. For the rest of us, we move on to the highly anticipated hands-on portion of the course known as "live tissue and trauma lanes." This phase of training is what truly separates Special Operations medics from other pre-hospital medical training programs. This type of training has been met with controversy. The fact is, this type of training has saved countless lives, not just on the battlefield, but here at home.

Before we conduct any training on the animals, a considerable amount of time is spent learning their anatomy. Every precaution is taken so they feel absolutely no pain or discomfort. We administer a heavy sedative before intubating. From this point forward, we're not allowed to refer to the patient as a goat; we're instructed they're a nine-year-old child and are to be treated as such. Over the next two weeks, I don't see a single incident involving the disrespect or abuse of the patients. As expected from this group, every member of our class conducts themselves with the highest degree of professionalism.

The first week is general skills. We're divided into four-man teams. Each team receives a new patient each day. We each do a series of four to five surgical procedures starting with the least invasive and work our way to more invasive. We do our best to put into action the procedures we practiced on mannequins in the preceding weeks. We make use of the external carotid arteries and use the smaller vessels to practice the venous cut down, which involves cutting and blunt dissecting the tissue around a vein in order to expose it. This is necessary in the event that peripheral venous access cannot be obtained and fluids have to be administered intravenously.

I lose count of the number of surgical cricothyrotomy and tracheostomies performed this week. Multiple chest tubes are performed each day before finishing each day with a hemorrhage lab. An instructor severs a major artery and yells, "Medic!" The student is responsible for stopping the active bleed in seconds. The ability to perform this skill alone has saved the lives of countless human beings, including enemy combatants.

The following week we're tested on each of the skills. Most of the class performs well through this phase, due largely to the way the course is taught. Hands-on repetition in a real-world setting is a format we're all comfortable with. Unlike the forty hours a week of mind-numbing death by PowerPoint in the previous section, we all take to the outdoor heat of the North Carolina summer and the sticky feel of real blood on our hands.

On the final day, we take the caprine to the incinerator. As we're stacking them in, in a thick accent, one of the German Special Forces soldiers makes the comment, "If we stack them more like this, we can fit more in." Our jaws drop to the floor and Adam, who's reclassing from Special Forces Weapons Sergeant, bursts into laughter so hard he literally falls to the ground. Within an instant the rest of us follow suit. Tears roll from my eyes as I attempt to catch my breath. Our six-foot-four German friend has no clue why we're laughing.

"What is funny?" he asks earnestly.

"You're fucking joking, right?"

"No, what is funny?"

"Oh, I don't know, maybe the German guy giving advice on how to fit more bodies into an incinerator? Come on man! Your military has some experience in that kind of thing, do they?" Adam replies in tears.

We can see the embarrassment in his eyes. He didn't think about it in that way at all.

He replies coldly with embarrassment, "We don't speak of that time in our history."

"What do you mean you don't speak of it?" asks one of the SEALs.

"It is taboo, we don't discuss it."

Not one among us feels bad about busting his balls. Later that night we buy him a beer and continue to joke with him about it. It's his first experience with the particular coarse brand of the American soldier's sense of humor. Humor is the coffee in a soldier's cup; the darker the blend, the greater the morale boost.

With live tissue training complete, it's time to move on to the most physically demanding part of the Special Operations Medic Course. We spend each day for the next three weeks in the sweltering heat of the North Carolina woods. Evolution after countless evolution is dedicated to making every step to treating a severely injured soldier automatic. Every possible scenario, every imaginable injury, is covered by our instructors, guys who've been operating as Special Ops medics for years.

No matter how much blood or how loud the screaming, it's imperative to create tranquility in the din of chaos. It must become effortless muscle memory. It's not good enough to be good; this is our bread and butter.

Trauma patient evaluation is the opus of the combat medic. Every bit of didactic and hands-on training culminates in a single thirty-minute assessment of our ability to perform in an austere environment. Our existence is defined by the actions we take when we hear that one terrifying word cried out.

"MEDIC!"

I hear the scream from within the woodline. This is it; time starts on my final practical hands-on exam for trauma lanes. The next thirty minutes will determine if I advance to the one-month clinical rotation, or I wash out. There's three hundred points total. Within those three hundred points, there's a handful of immediate disqualifiers or "No-Go's" if missed.

I respond to the call, running eighty meters into the woods. I find my patient lying face-up, covered in fake blood. The trauma management sequence flows from my mouth like the Pledge of Allegiance did in first grade. It's burned into my memory. My hands complete each movement as my mouth describes in detail what I'm doing to my instructor, who is standing over me with a clipboard.

"BSI, scene is safe, I have one patient, Haji and I can handle . . ."

The instructor echoes back, "Scene is safe, you have one patient, no further assistance needed."

"Buddy? Buddy are you okay?"

"Your patient responds with a moan and says it hurts."

"Where does it hurt?

"My chest."

"Do you know where you are?"

"Patient responds, 'I'm in the woods.'"

"Do you know your name and rank?"

"Patient responds, 'Sergeant Smith.'"

"Do you know how long you've been hurt?"

"I've been here for less than ten minutes."

"Patient is alert and oriented to person, place, and time."

I check for any major life threats such as arterial bleeds. I rule out airway obstructions since he's communicating with me verbally. My rapid blood sweep reveals bright red blood squirting from the patient's left inner thigh. I pull the makeshift windlass tourniquet from my bag. Even though there's much more advanced versions of this device, we're required to make our own out of sticks and cravats. In fact, most of the items in my aid bag at the schoolhouse is handmade. It demands resourcefulness. Plus, if you can get hemorrhage control with an antiquated old napkin, achieving it with a fancy CAT2 or ratchet tourniquet should be a breeze.

Tourniquet is in place. I call out, "I have homeostasis!"

My instructor pulls on the tourniquet to make sure it's in place. "You have homeostasis."

There are critical criteria which must be met under specific time limits. I make the first time cut-off for controlling major life threats and move on. The assessment continues with airway, breathing, and circulation. My patient also has a tension pneumothorax, which means his lung is popped and the air in his pleural cavity is keeping the lung from expanding fully. The immediate treatment involves taking a massive needle and placing it between the ribs just below the collarbone to release the tension. I make it through the primary assessment and package the patient for movement. I transport the patient to our makeshift Combat Support Hospital or CSH (pronounced "cash").

The long-term treatment for a tension pneumothorax is to place a chest tube, also known as tube thoracostomy. This requires placing a tube the diameter of your thumb between the fifth and sixth rib directly under the armpit. Since no one I've ever met would ever volunteer for this procedure, we're required to verbally walk the instructor through each point. Everyone who's made it this far in the course has displayed proficiency on this procedure in live tissue phase numerous times.

Thankfully, placement of the Foley catheter is another procedure we talk through, for the most part. We're required to start the procedure using our buddy's actual penis. Cleaning the site with iodine and preparing for the placement of a huge plastic tube. Imagine being in a tent in the woods with a man standing over your shoulder with a clipboard and having to gorilla grip your best friend's dick in one hand and swab the head till it's orange with the other. It's not gay, it's medicine.

Right before insertion, we're allowed to trade out for what we call "The Stunt Cock!" Most guys make their own out of a container we commonly use to place used needles in called a "sharps shuttle." Nothing too fancy, just a container to slide the Foley tube in. One of the guys transferring from Ranger Battalion to Special Forces testing out on the lane next to me put a significant amount of time into his, though.

It's massive! It's the size of a bottle of Jameson at least, complete with huge nut sack. He even used IV tubing to make it appear veiny. I can't help but laugh when he pulls out the massive fake dick. It creates welcome levity in the middle of a stressful test.

One of the final procedures we're required to perform is the Digital Rectal Exam or DRE. Yep, we now have to put our finger into our buddy's ass again, this time to check for bleeding.

The dreaded time during our trauma lane assessment for me to check my buddy for intestinal bleeding has come. Remembering the psychological trauma I sustained from Jake the finger twirler, I decide to fake it. We're told beforehand if anyone is caught faking this procedure they'll have to demonstrate proficiency on themselves in front of the rest of the class, so I'm taking a pretty big risk in not going three knuckles deep. I told my partner beforehand if he wants to avoid the mild molestation, then he will grit his teeth and act like a man who's getting penetrated when the time comes.

Success. The instructor doesn't notice when I fold my index finger and fake the funk. It's the last skill on my assessment. I call time and look to my instructor; he just shakes his head. My heart sinks deep into my guts. *What did I forget?* He signals me over to meet him outside of the CSH.

"So, Ranger, what went wrong?" he asks.

"Nothing, Sergeant, I thought I did everything I was supposed to."

"Oh, so you think your shit was perfect, huh? Three hundred out of three hundred? You're so fucking shit-hot that you didn't miss one single thing? Is that what you think, Ranger?"

Now not only did I fail the most important test of this course, my teacher thinks I'm an arrogant prick. I take in a deep breath and brace for impact.

"Well," he says, "you'd be right. Three hundred."

Holy fucking shit! I almost don't believe him. This is the biggest hurdle thrown at you in this course and I just passed it! It's like a two-ton stone is lifted off my shoulders. I grow six inches taller in the moment. I still have to make it through a month-long clinical rotation and a handful of other tests including the National Registry exam for Paramedic, but I just made it over the highest mountain in this course.

About a week after Jake accosted me during the initial DRE, we were tested on nasogastric tube. An NG tube is a long, skinny tube inserted into the stomach via the nose. We were instructed not to consume any food prior to practicing this procedure because it is known to create a significant gag response. Knowing Jake was once again going to be my partner, I decide it's the appropriate time for reprisal. I ate a half a dozen scrambled eggs with salsa, a huge glass of milk, and some yogurt right before the procedure. We sit up in a chair while our partners feed the three-foot-long tube down our noses. As the gagging begins, I become overjoyed. Jake got to wear the smell of my untimely snack for the rest of the morning.

The most anticipated part of the SOMC course is the trauma rotations. We're integrated into a hospital and ambulance setting where we're able to apply all of the skills we've learned over the previous five months. There's three different locations for students to go. I'm sent to Bayfront Hospital in Tampa, Florida. We travel by bus from Ft. Bragg and arrive in the middle of the night. We're set to report to the hospital first thing the next morning, but as one keen observer on the bus notices, "it's only midnight and there's a bar right next to our condos." Whiskey Joe's. The establishment takes a substantial amount of my pay for the month.

The next morning, we arrive at the hospital just after sunrise. We haven't even set our bags down yet when a call comes through saying there's a gunshot victim en route. We're going to be working in a three-man team under the direction of the Medical Doctor on duty.

Thirty seconds into the start of our trauma rotation and the three of us are about to work an actual gunshot wound. One of us is responsible for establishing an airway, the other an additional IV line, and I end up with "any other" procedures. When the patient rolls in, I hesitate mildly. It's not a fit male in his early twenties. For months we've only worked on each other and for the most part, we all pretty much have the same anatomical landmarks. Ironically, our first patient is an extremely obese female. She's bleeding from her abdomen, her clothes cut away by the civilian paramedics.

The two Marine Recon Corpsmen who are in charge of airway and circulation jump right in. I'm impressed as usual with how they handle the situation, a true credit to their unit. Marine Recon Corpsmen don't get enough credit in the Special Operations community. I believe they're some of the most squared-away guys I've ever worked with. I, on the other hand, am at a bit of a loss as to what my role is supposed to be.

The nurse informs me the patient requires a Foley catheter. I'm sure the look on my face in this moment is priceless. This isn't a stunt cock. In fact, the anatomy is completely different than what I've trained for. There's copious amounts of blood and more flaps and folds of fat than I've ever seen. The head nurse instructs me, "Go on, get in there."

Well then, go on asshole . . . lead the way, I think to myself.

I must've spent five minutes trying to get that fucking tube in place. Jamming and forcing my way through the heinous stink and unrecognizable terrain features. By the time the sweat pours down my face, the nurse jumps in and saves me. In a smart ass tone she comments, "Don't worry, Soldier, it happens to lots of guys their first time." I know it's going to be a long month.

The rotation is divided between the hospital and prehospital environment. In order to meet the National Registry of EMT's requirement for paramedic, we spend several days working alongside the city's busiest paramedics. We're also required to conduct procedures in several of the hospital's departments, including assisting deliveries in the OB GYN, setting casts with the Ortho, and scrubbing in alongside the surgeons in the operating room.

Through the course of my time at the hospital in Florida, I'm able to scrub in on half a dozen trauma surgeries. One of which, the surgeon accidentally stabs my small finger with the dirty suture needle he's using to sew together the intestines of a man shot in the abdomen. "Just pour some hydrogen peroxide on it, you'll be fine," is his suggestion. I opt for a blood test and two weeks of antiretrovirals instead.

I assist in the delivery of four babies, one by cesarean section. I place limbs in casts and stitch up every part of the human body that you can imagine. One gentlemen is rolled into the emergency room whose throat was diced and hacked like he'd been attacked by a shark. Apparently he got in an argument with his neighbor who pulled a box cutter on him and used it without hesitation. His trachea and carotid artery are completely exposed, but undamaged. His sternocleidomastoid (muscle of the neck) is severed and rolled up under his jaw.

Two of us put over a hundred stitches in his neck and chest. Miraculously, the man is awake and talking to us the entire time. A testament to how resilient the human body truly is. The amount of abuse a body is able to take and continue functioning is nothing short of miraculous.

My stitching buddy for the next two hours is Brian. He's one of the Marine Recon medics on the clinical rotation. He's a smart guy, quiet more often than not, and has been in the Navy for several years before attending the SOMC. He jokes with the man as we work on his neck and chest. When the man asks how he looks, Brian just replies, "You aren't going to be winning any beauty pageants, but you're still alive."

I do central lines and intubations, work on people having heart attacks and drunken homeless people who've been stabbed. I sew a man's ear back on and stitch another guy's skull who was attacked by his girlfriend's six-inch stiletto heel. Despite the action, boredom still manages to creep in around 4:00 a.m.

I walk into one of the trauma rooms late one evening toward the end of our shift to discover a couple of my classmates playing with the defibrillator.

They placed the large electrode on one of the guy's arms and are firing it at a low level. The result being the contraction of the biceps muscle, and in turn, the flexing of the elbow. Of course, as soon as I see this immature, unsafe fooling around while we're supposed to be working, I'm forced to interject, "Oh man, let me try."

"Hold on, we're going to put them on Kip's thigh." The result is the same as the upper arm; the quad contracts, resulting in extension at the knee. All the while we laugh like children.

"Let's try it on the pecs," someone suggests.

"I think that would actually shock your heart, though."

"Oh yeah, good call. Where else can we go with this?"

"I have an idea," I reply. I take the two palm-size electrodes and slap one on each of my ass cheeks. "Let's see about this." Up until this point, we've been using an energy level of about twenty joules. The man at the helm gets a crazy look in his eyes just as I place my hands on the hospital bed. He sets the machine to a hundred joules and fires it off. The result is the most intense muscular glute contraction I've ever experienced, nearly sending me over the bed.

"Yeaaayaa huumfh." I manage to wince, in a kind of a sound you only make when something painful is also a little exciting. The 4:00 a.m. silence of the emergency room is shattered by the laughter of my peers. He looks at me again and I look back into his reckless eyes. His hand on the knob, I know his intentions; I'd do the same.

"No," I say timidly, while shaking my head. No dice. He's committed. He cranks the machine up to two hundred before I can pull the pads off my ass.

ZZZZZZZaaaaaaapp.

"Ugggghhhh fuugggin tykaaa!" The jolt takes me completely off of my feet and again the room bursts into laughter. The series of sounds emanating from behind the closed door pique the curiosity of the nurses sitting at their respective stations. One enters to see me, pants around my ankles, dick in hand, electrodes stuck to my bare white ass, with the traumatized look of electric shock therapy on my face. My friends laughing so hard they've stopped making noise. It's that painful kind of laughter you want to stop just long enough to take a breath.

"What in the . . ." is all she can muster. Another nurse immediately peers over her right shoulder.

"You guys are insane," the second nurse chimes in. My friend turns the power on the machine back down under a hundred and commences a series of shocks which cause me to dance around the room. Everyone, including the nurses, are in a helpless fit of laughter now. "We should all hang out sometime," she concludes after catching her breath.

The problem is, we've only got a couple of nights off the entire month. Most of the guys willing to have extracurricular time with the nurses sacrifice the little sleep time we have. On our first free night of the rotation, I'm much more motivated by the premise of posting up at a dive bar and attempt to break my previous beer record of twenty-four in a single evening.

Jake, one of my friends in the Special Forces pipeline, has a different plan, though. He's friendly with a very attractive girl whose name I don't bother to learn. Jake puts himself in a tough spot because he just signed out the keys to the van to take his lady friend out. However, there's six of us with the night off and he's required to take us where we need to go. He decides to try to make everyone happy by inviting us all out to dinner with the promise of going to a bar. He tells ol' girl they'll be going out on a date. I don't believe he mentions to her the addition of a squad of sophomoric Special Operations guys looking to get drunk.

He takes us to a nice restaurant at the marina where they charge six dollars for a beer. I don't want to be here. I want to be at the dive bar. I become increasingly troublesome, making obscene jokes and attempting to light the tablecloth on fire with the centerpiece candle, right in front of the waiter. Now you might think that's terrible behavior for a grown man, and it is; however, I was led to this place under the guise we'd be going to a slummed-out hole in the wall.

Upon leaving the restaurant I notice a dive bar down the street with a neon Pabst Blue Ribbon sign, shining like a beacon to guide a lost sailor home. I'm not the only one in the group in need of some good old-fashioned bar stool therapy. We've all been elbows deep in blood and guts and could use a flick of the pressure release valve.

To my dismay, they don't even stock PBR. I ask the bearded gent behind the bar, "What's the shittiest beer you have here?" From under the bar he produces a can of Schlitz malt liquor and a small paper bag. With the grace and fluidity of a symphony conductor, he places the can in the small paper bag and hands it to me. I can feel the tears welling up as my lip quivers slightly. I'm so happy. So very, very happy.

Ten years later, the very same paper bag is still folded neatly in my wallet. Every time I've consumed a Schlitz since that day, I pull out that bag and used it like the ghetto koozie it is.

After consuming enough malt liquor to float a ship, it's time to "break the seal." During SOMC I learn the need to pee more frequently is a hormone reaction. Alcohol inhibits the production and secretion of antidiuretic hormone (ADH), which causes more frequent urination. To this day, I have no clue what motivates my next action, aside from possibly the interaction the nearly two dozen drinks is having on my decision-making process.

In the men's room, I grab a fistful of brown paper towels and remove the splash guard from the urinal I'm about to take a piss in. I place the wad of towels containing the rubber treasure deep into my cargo pocket and return to my barstool without a word. We continue libating for another half an hour until someone suggests getting ice cream across the street.

Earlier in the week I met a girl at a restaurant who gave me her number. She has the bad timing of calling me at this very moment.

"Hey, Leo, I'm off and going out to the bar with a couple of friends if you're interested in joining us." I present the invitation to the rowdy, drunken group of bachelors. Needless to say, it's not a hard sell for the group. We get our ice cream to go, but not before engaging in an epic mini-plastic-sword fight which leaves two of us bleeding from the fingers.

When we arrive at the new bar, we each grab another drink and meet the girls at their table. I'm swaying in my seat as the world moves around me. We make small talk, but I get bored quickly. Just as I have no idea why I decided to grab that nasty splash guard out of the urinal, I have no clue why I believe it's a good idea to retrieve the wad of brown paper towels from my pocket at this moment. I hand them to the girl who invited us and say, "Here . . . I got you something."

Brian takes an interest in the exchange, watching intently as she unwraps the mystery gift, her face marked with anticipation. The thoughtfulness of a guy she hardly knows considerate enough to bring her a gift. She's certainly not expecting a gift, so she's rather excited by the surprise. When all of the paper is removed, she holds the diamond-shaped, red piece of rubber in her bare hands with a perplexed look on her face. Brian's eyes triple in size as he realizes what it is. It's that look you expect a bystander to give if you kick a baby for no reason. Mortified. He tries to control his laughter, but the fact she still has no clue what she's holding is too much for him. He erupts, tears filling his eyes. Now she's really confused. I lean over and tell her, "Any asshole can bring you flowers. How's that for original?"

"Jesus Christ, Jenkins!" replies another buddy once he realizes what's going on. He tells her what she's holding is what keeps piss from splashing back on your hands at the urinal. To everyone's surprise, she starts laughing. She looks at me and says, "That's funny. Disgusting, but funny."

At the end of the evening we discover one of the ladies we've been hanging out with has a flat tire. Seizing the white knight opportunity to help the woman he's interested in, one of my buddies removes his shirt and crawls under her car. He gets filthy in the process, but gets the spare on. Apparently, watching the Special Forces Soldier remove his top and get sweaty changing a tire was game over for her. Years later, the two get married and to my knowledge, her friend kept the highly inappropriate, yet perfectly unique gift for years.

There's no other training in the world that can compare to it. It's the most comprehensive, progressive program for trauma medics on earth. By the end of SOMC I feel prepared to handle any potential injury on the field of battle. Which is a good thing, because within two weeks of graduating, I'm sent back to Ft. Benning and deploy to Afghanistan to act as a platoon medic for Charlie Company, 3rd Ranger Battalion.

Drinking from a firehose! The books
assigned to us on the first day of SOMC.

Extreme log PT at the schoolhouse. Tony Mena on a 6-mile stroll
through Ft. Bragg with over 100 lbs. to carry before class starts.

SOMC graduation.

CHAPTER 6

Time Consumer

*"I think a curse should rest on me—because I love this war. I know it's
smashing and shattering the lives of thousands every moment, and yet,
I can't help it, I enjoy every second of it."*
Winston Churchill

It's fall of 2004. I've been a soldier in the United States Army for eighteen
months. Most of the guys I went to basic training with have already
deployed to Iraq or Afghanistan, while I've spent the last year and a half in
various schools preparing to be a member of Special Operations. Every hurdle
bounded gives me an increased level of confidence in my ability to operate
among the world's best soldiers. Every crucible passed is a necessary evolution
to belonging to a unit of this caliber.

All of that confidence is stripped away when I take my first step off the
back of the Air Force cargo plane onto the runway of Bagram Airfield. The
mountains surrounding the airfield show me how insignificant I am. I've done
a considerable amount of hiking growing up in Arizona, but my perspective
on what a mountain is changes instantly as my size ten and a half combat
boots hit the tarmac.

My eyes stretch wide in awe. I can feel the brisk sting of the cold, dry air.
My lungs fill with something different, almost ancient. In all my travels before

and since, I've never smelled that same smell, except for the two other times I step off of a plane, back in time, and onto Afghan soil.

A desperate uncertainty seeps in as I realize I'm not entirely sure what my exact role is here. I know I'm the medic, but what does that mean? I've been immersed in medical training so long, I haven't even fired a rifle for almost a year and a half, and that was the no frills, M16 in basic training. Add to this, I don't know a single person who I'll be working with. My entire battalion deployed a month earlier, and I've never met any of them. I'm the FNG (Fucking New Guy). None of my accomplishments up to this point mean a damn thing. No one knows me. I have to prove my proficiency all over again.

On my very first day in country I'm attached to who I believe will be my platoon. We conduct fast rope training together. The act is simple enough; grab the rope dangling from the back of the helicopter and slide down it like a fire pole. This, however, is literally the first time I've ever actually been in a helicopter, which adds heavily to the anxiety I'm already experiencing. On one of the final evolutions of the day, one of the squad leaders badly sprains his ankle.

An ankle sprain? I didn't expect this to be my first patient as a Ranger medic. I prepared for gunshot wounds, and bones sticking out, and giant stunt cocks. The majority of the training at the schoolhouse is targeted at the worst possible scenario. He honestly would've been better off being shot.

I freeze up a bit. The trauma assessment sequence buzzes through my head, but there's no need for it. He doesn't need me to check his airway or start an IV. There's no major life threats or hemorrhaging to control. My aid bag isn't packed to treat this injury. I have some pain meds, but I don't have the right size needles to do a simple intramuscular injection. This is more like a sick call injury, not what I expect to see in the field. The experienced Staff Sergeant screams in pain as I plunged an 18-gauge needle into the meat of his shoulder.

"Fuck, Doc! I feel like I just got arm raped! Do you even know what the fuck you're doing?"

I want to tell him how good I did on my trauma lane in SOMC, or how praised I was by the doctors during my hospital rotation, but none of that shit matters here. I'm fucking this up bad. I wrap his ankle the way you'd expect a monkey to if you threw a splint and a couple of bananas in his cage. I'm a fucking soup sandwich. With the help of another Ranger, I get the pissed off squad leader to the clinic and brace for the worst.

Miraculously, before he's released, I'm assigned to another platoon at another forward operating base (FOB). If I had to stay and work as that man's medic for the next three months, I would've been in serious trouble. Instead, I get a second helo ride, this time over the seemingly endless, snow-covered mountains of majestic Afghanistan.

I arrive at my home, FOB Salerno. There's already two other Ranger platoons here from my company. I stand in a small formation with a dozen other new guys. The process of deciding who goes to each platoon is not what I imagined on the long flight from Georgia. The Platoon Sergeants stand in front of the wide-eyed new Rangers and begin a selection process I can only compare to picking teams for a game of grade school kickball.

There's no inquiry or interview. "He looks strong, I'll take him." Like cattle at a livestock auction. I'm beginning to become incredibly self-conscious about not getting picked in the first three rounds when I realize all of the non-infantry guys have been put in the back row for a reason. Our fate has already been decided. We will become the property of our section leaders. Mine is a six-foot tall gentleman with a shaved head and a full leg piece tattoo. *Awesome, another Runza*. I think to myself. In the deepest voice you can possibly imagine he yells my name.

"JENKINS, over here!"

The guy I have to report to from here out looks like the poster child for the Aryan race. Dano, as he's known to everyone who isn't a cherry fuck like me, is the epitome of what I've always imagined a Ranger to be. His demeanor is beyond intimidating. There's no hesitation in his character. Ice flows through his calloused veins, standing here in the foreground of a dusty war zone.

There's a steep learning curve to being a Ranger. I have eighteen months of training, but no real perspective as to what day-to-day life is like. Minutes after meeting my new senior medic, I learn that partially being a special operations medic looks like four cots in the back of a tent serving as the medical facility for two platoons of injury-prone guys thousands of miles from their moms. I'm shown which one of the cots is my new home, drop the bag I'll be living out of for the next few months, and receive a short tour of the base.

The other new Rangers I arrive with are having a more tumultuous introduction into the Regiment, most of whom are infantrymen, and have only been in the Army about five months. The look on some of their faces at the chow hall later in the day resemble the look a dog has right after it's been kicked for shitting in the house.

On our first evening, First Sergeant Sealy gathers us into one of the tents to give us a brief introduction to the area. 1SG is nicknamed "The Rhino," and for good reason. The man's arms are bigger around than my legs and he possesses a palpable confidence, even amongst other Rangers. He commands respect in all environments.

The Company Commander also introduces himself during the meeting, gives a short speech, and opens the floor for any questions. During the course of his introduction the CO tells us his background, including his alma mater, The Citadel.

Things are going fine in our introduction until the CO opens the floor for questions. One of the privates, who we will call "Maldo," has a burning desire to know some things about the CO's school. I don't think much of it when he asks, "Sir, is it true that you have to pee in the sink at the Citadel?"

With the grace and composure of a veteran Ranger, the CO explains, "In many of the dorms, the bathrooms are far apart and sometimes you have to improvise." The CO then calmly leaves us in the care of "The Rhino." To this day I'm still not sure if he screamed "GET OUT" or "GET DOWN;" all I know is it's nothing but assholes and elbows. The 1SG didn't find the inquiry very humorous and he let us know in his own unique way. After a very shitty twenty minutes in that tent, we're brought out into the cold night air and made to create a small formation.

Our respective section leaders are brought out and informed about what just occurred. I'm introduced to the taste of Afghan dirt as I low crawl to the tent which acts as our communications room and armory. I'm issued my night vision goggles (NVGs) in the front leaning rest position, feet elevated on a desk. At this moment, I can't help but think back to the schoolhouse at

Ft. Bragg, where just a couple of weeks ago I was having a barbecue with Master Sergeants, joking and calling them by their first names. Now I'm pulling myself across the ground in a war zone because someone who I've never met asked a smartass question to another guy I've never met. Welcome to Ranger Battalion.

My first week is a series of tests. My senior medic quizzes me randomly on drug protocols and assessment techniques. He takes me out on a death run in hopes I will fall off his pace. The fact I've been obsessed with physical fitness before this and spend at least a couple of hours a day training pays off. By showing I'm fit to fight on my first few days, I display personal responsible and partial trustworthiness. The military works differently than the rest of the world. I've always said success here relies heavily on three things: be in good physical condition, be early for everything, and maintain a clean, well-groomed appearance. It's not long before I fuck one of those three things up.

I'm watching a movie on a shitty 13-inch TV in my tent when a young private runs in. Out of breath, he frantically tells me, "Dano is looking for you; you're late for a training meeting."

"Training meeting? No one told me about a—"

"Doc, come on!"

When I arrive at the headquarters tent everyone is on a study break. My boss looks at me like he's trying to melt my face with his eyes. He's fucking pissed. The First Sergeant tells everyone to take their seats. Apparently we're halfway through a two-hour PowerPoint presentation I was completely unaware of. You see, the military has a deliberate chain of command. The First Sergeant tells his platoon sergeants, they tell their squad leaders, the squad leaders pass it on to their team leaders, the team leaders scream it at their privates while making them do push-ups. It's highly effective except no one ever thinks to tell the medic what the fuck is going on. I didn't blow this training off; I simply didn't know it was happening. That doesn't matter. When the training ends everyone else leaves the tent to go on with their day. I and the other platoon medic, Matt, who's also unaware of the presentation, get to stay back for some "extra training."

We attempt to explain that no one told us what's going on while sweating buckets in the front leaning rest position. Our senior medic says something simple which sticks with me to this day.

"This is your company. It's your responsibility to know what's going on without someone telling you. You have to be proactive, not reactive, or you won't survive here." It's one of the most valuable lessons of my first combat deployment.

The days begin to smear together. Succotash. Again. The waxy lima beans and flavorless corn occupy the upper right corner of my Styrofoam tray. A sort of flank steak with a density far exceeding the plastic instruments intended to dissect it is the main course. I haven't gone back to the salad bar since Dano nearly died from ingesting some of the fecal matter on the brown iceberg lettuce. It's this or an MRE, and I've already gone that route several times this week.

Our dining facility is a dingy white tent illuminated by the struggling generators constantly buzzing just outside the front entrance. The large white tent sits in the middle of the small FOB, just outside of the town of Khost, Afghanistan.

The boys sit around the table and tell jokes for several minutes after choking down their dinner. The billowing laugh of First Sergeant Sealy is enough to drown out the irritating noise coming from the generators. I'm still leery of the big man at this point after our initial encounter.

I tread lightly in my comments as we leave the chow hall under the guidance of our red head lamps. The camp stays blacked out at night. Using white lights has the potential to draw RPG fire, so we stumble around making due with the minimal illumination from the red filtered lights. My home is now a bunk bed in the corner of a tent I share with eight other Rangers. My senior medic believes moving in with a squad will help with my integration as a platoon medic. Our tent is equipped with a 19" TV one of the guys purchased from the bazaar prior to my arrival in country. The squad leader and Alpha team leader are both big poker players, so the back part of our tent is set up like a miniature casino, frequently hosting company poker nights.

After dinner is down time. Typically we spend evenings watching very poor quality movies purchased at the market for a dollar. More often than not, I make my way back to the gym for the second or third time of the day. The gym is the only place I feel at home these days. Everywhere else I'm the new guy in the company, but on that dirt-floored, musty, old building, I'm one of the strongest guys in our company. The rattling of ancient rusted iron plates, likely left behind when the Russians occupied the country, sound more to me like the light chatter at the breakfast table of the firehouse where I used to work. The gym becomes my sanctuary from both the monotony and chaos of war.

There isn't a great deal of activity in our area at this time. I believe it's Ramadan, and as a result, most of the local terrorists are on vacation. After over a year and a half in the Army, it comes time for my first mission. It's pitch black and I find myself sitting in the back of a Humvee with no armor; it doesn't even have doors. I have no idea what to expect and beyond that, I have no clue how to work my NVGs. The last time I put a round in an M4 was . . . actually never. We qualified with an M16 in basic training a year and a half earlier, but I haven't fired a weapon since. My class was the last RIP class that didn't have a shooting week (December 2003). As I hear some of the other guys yelling in jest at the guy who opens the gate at the FOB, "I'm scared" . . . "I wanna be a princess" . . . "It's too cold out here!" I'm trying desperately to figure out how to get the bullet from the magazine into the fucking barrel.

The jeep bounces and jars the bones of its occupants on the two-hour drive to the objective. Green beams project into every direction from the PEQ-2 lasers mounted on our M4s as we scan for potential threats in the distance. We very quietly arrive at the base of a hill, atop of which sits a secure compound barely visible in the minimal moonlight. In silence, we dismount and begin to pull security in each direction. I'm instructed by the platoon sergeant to come with him.

Our element begins to make its way up the incline in the darkness. The single night vision device bangs against my cheekbone while displaying a very blurry green image. I've never worn these things before, let alone attempted to walk on uneven terrain with them. There's no depth perception and I stumble, letting out an audible grunt.

"Quite, Doc!" aggressively whispers one of the unidentifiable members of my platoon.

The laborious walk takes about fifteen minutes. I'm staged outside the front gate as the assault element breaches the door and begins to clear the central courtyard. In less than a minute, I'm brought into the compound. I look around to see Rangers moving swiftly and silently from building to building, collecting fighting age males and securing the women and children in a single room. I can't help but think how fucking cool the entire thing is. I finally get to see exactly what Rangers actually do. Not what I've read in books or heard stories about, but how they actually move with grace and fluidity, subduing their opponents with a certain violent professionalism.

I'm given the task of watching the room of noncombatants after the dust has settled on the initial assault. I put on several layers in anticipation of the frigid Humvee infill, but the movement to the objective left me sweating. The room where I watch over the dozen or so women and children couldn't be hotter. I remove my helmet and hooded face mask. The older women in the room appear startled and chatter among themselves. I ask the interpreter what they're saying. Apparently my blonde hair and face resemble the Russian soldiers who occupied this region years before. I find out from the terp that the Russians were not very kind to the women when they were here. I see the look of concern spreading throughout the room. *What an absolutely terrifying experience for these little kids!* Twenty minutes ago they're sound asleep in their beds and now they have a man in body armor standing over them with a rifle.

I remember I have a bag of candy in my cargo pocket. Every eye in the room is glued attentively to my movement as I reach into my pocket and pull out the zip lock bag. I kneel down and offer a piece to the closest child in the room. She's an absolutely adorable little girl, maybe four or five years old. Her brown hair is matted and wild. Her facial expression is curious. In her little nightgown, she hesitantly reaches for the brightly wrapped treasure at my fingertips. Like a little mouse who just secured the cheese from a trap, she retreats back to the safety of the group.

This sets off a reaction one may expect from any group of small children when candy is being dispensed, regardless of nationality. I instantly become the most popular person in the province. I hand out every one of those sugary treats and can't help but think about my young nieces back home. Just as I receive the call for exfil, the first brave little girl comes back to me and tugs on my pant leg. She hands me a brown necklace I later give to my niece, Hailey.

As we make our way out of the compound, I walk through the outdoor kitchen. The walls are stained with soot and it has an almost ancient smell. The burnt iron kettle suspended from a hook reminds me of something that would have been used hundreds, if not thousands of years ago. I come to find out the majority of the country is caught in some sort of a time warp. Much of the technology and culture has not progressed beyond biblical times, like a sort of time capsule allowing us to look into our past.

The drive back to Salerno is just as miserable as the trip to the objective. By the time we roll into the security of the gates I can no longer feel my hands. We conduct a quick check for sensitive items and dust off our equipment. The thing about Afghanistan is you can try to get clean but you will always be covered in dirt. Very little of the country is paved and riding in the back of what is essentially a pickup truck will leave every part of you filthy. It's of little concern to me. I haven't spoken with my family since I arrived. We only have two working phones for the five dozen Rangers here, but I know there won't be a wait for either of them right after a mission.

The MWR tent is a drafty hut with a shelf in the back with books and items delivered for nonspecific soldiers, letters from school kids and drawings, that sort of thing. There's four desks featuring layers of carvings, courtesy of the pocket knives carried by each of the Rangers who anxiously await their chance to speak with a loved one. Each one of the four has a phone, but only two of them ever worked.

I dial the staff duty number and ask to be patched through to my father's home line. The connection is shoddy at best. I'm not allowed to discuss anything I'm doing or where I am, but it's a relief to hear my father's voice. He tells me everything is good and nothing has changed at all. I find out later that's not true, but his protective instincts didn't want me being distracted by any bad news from back home. The call is short-lived. Someone outside the fence decides now is a good time to lob a mortar round at our compound. I'm not sure if the sirens wail first or the phone cut out. Either way, I'm sure that's the last thing my pops wanted to hear.

I exit the tent to see all of the guys running to the shelter of several concrete bunkers. Many of them are already dressed down for the evening, in little more than Ranger panties and body armor. The standard operating procedure is to meet in these little makeshift concrete caves until we get an all clear. We sit packed in like sardines for about thirty minutes before being allowed to return to our tents.

The next morning starts just like every other one for the next few months. With hygiene bag in tote, in a faded brown shirt and short black silky shorts, we move like zombies to the Conex-box-like latrines. Every step is more painful than the one before. The paper-thin shower shoes are no match for the jagged Afghan rocks. *Face shaved. Teeth brushed. Bowels cleared. Move out. Check in with the senior medic at the aid station to see if anyone is there for sick call. PFC Joe Snuffy has a sore knee. Here's some Motrin. Ninety minutes before the dingy white tent opens for breakfast, back to the gym. What day is it? Chest day, that's what day it is!*

I wonder what kind of eggs we will have today, runny or brick hard? Following breakfast, we're informed we're going to the range so the new guys can sight in their weapons. Since the last range I attended was in basic training, I have a preconceived notion what training will be like today. To my surprise, there's no tower, no pre-dug fox holes, and no gates. It's literally just an open field. We drive out to the desert and set up targets. This reminds me of all of the times we did the same thing growing up in Arizona. In fact, the terrain is almost identical to where we used to go as kids.

The experience is surprisingly laid-back. No one is shouting. After sighting in our weapons, we work on line drills where we walk one direction and shoot, then the next direction. Walk and shoot, run and shoot, turn and shoot, shoot and shoot. We shoot until my finger is blistered. We become familiar with every weapon system we have, including weapons commonly used by our enemies, such as the AK47.

We eat MREs for lunch and shoot into the early evening, an event we repeat on a weekly basis for the next few months. At night, after dinner, we return to our tents to enjoy another pirated movie. A half dozen of us huddle around the TV, sitting in camping chairs and sharing the bounty from the care packages that just came in. One particular delivery brought several cases of Girl Scout Cookies from Erik's mother. Knowing he can't possibly eat the dozens upon dozens of boxes himself, he shares the contents with his roommates.

Sundays are down days. One Sunday in particular, we decide to have a gangster marathon. We watch all three *Godfather* films, *Goodfellas*, and a myriad of other lesser quality movies. I personally take down six full boxes of Thin Mints between lunch and dinner that day. I regret nothing!

The days and nights blur together in a sort of war-fighter Groundhog Day. The only moments spent alone are the three or four minutes secluded in a porta potty with a porn magazine, illuminated by your red head lamp. It's sick to say, but I still get a little excited when I see red lights.

Wake up. Shave face. Lift weights. Eat breakfast. Shoot. Eat lunch. Practice CQB. Eat dinner. Lift weights. Watch a movie. Take your anti-malaria pill. Go to bed. Repeat. With any group of highly motivated, barrel-chested freedom fighters, boredom is a very dangerous thing. Idle hands are the devil's playthings, as they say, and no one is more familiar than we are.

For most, a birthday is a time of celebration, a time to bring attention to yourself and the things you've accomplished over the past year. In Ranger Battalion, it is a cause for torture. For that reason, most guys will purposely let the day come and go without mention. Occasionally you will have a friend known as a Blue Falcon (BF= Buddy Fucker) who will tell the rest of your platoon it's your special day.

One unfortunate soul believed he was going to make it through the entire day without incident. However, we maintained different plans and were plotting his demise for most of the week. It's close to Christmas time now. We're watching movies in one of the other squad's tents. We have a brief intermission between films for a quick bathroom break. The birthday boy dons his red head lamp and walks the two hundred meters to the outhouse.

Our six-man element quickly reacts without hesitation. As the target fades into the night, the squad of Rangers affixes their NVGs and removes any colorful clothing, replacing it with all-black base layer. Mobilizing into blocking positions, we block any potential means of egress the enemy may think to take. We wait in silence in the freezing cold dark night for him to reemerge from the row of shitters.

Waiting patiently for him to get right in the middle of our formation, we peer through the darkness. He is completely oblivious of our whereabouts.

As he draws closer, "CONTACT! CONTACT! CONTACT!"

One of the privates rushes at him, wrapping him up. Two more pile on. He's no match for this level of violence of action. Before he knows what's happening he's on the ground and being zip-tied. He never had a chance. One of the senior privates produces a fresh can of shaving cream and begins to go to work on the detainee. Another grabs a case of bottled water and douses him to his bones. The man is violently dragged to a nearby chain link fence and tied to it. We sing *Happy Birthday* as we return to the warmth of our tent, leaving the drenched man to tolerate the freezing Afghan night. About halfway through the second movie someone remembers he's still outside. "Ohh yeah! Meh, we'll get him after this is done."

The way that Thanksgiving came and went, so did Christmas and New Year's. By the time our rotation ends in early 2005, I manage to gain the respect of the men around me. I realize, however, that there's hundreds more men in the Battalion who I haven't met. When we return, I will once again be the new guy. I will have to prove myself to them as well.

This is the nature of life in Ranger Battalion. There's no place for a guy who rests on his laurels. If you're a good team leader, you have to prove yourself as a good squad leader and then as a platoon sergeant and so on. Battalion is a constant proving ground where you're expected to be at your absolute best on a daily basis. Every day may not be an action-packed gun fight the way it's depicted in movies, but the highest standard is the expectation, every day and on every task. That consistency in expectation is what makes the highest caliber of warrior.

When it's time to go home, I envision the scene I watched time and time again on television. A group of service members land on some runway and are greeted with crowds of loved ones waving flags and welcome home signs. That doesn't happen. Not even close. We land on a military base in the middle of the night, walk into a hangar where three young medics give out shots, take a short bus ride to our company area, turn in weapons, and go home. It's the most unceremonious evening imaginable.

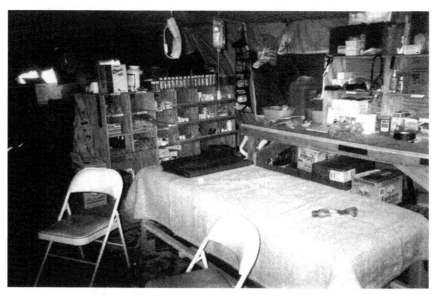

The aid station at FOB Salerno, winter 2004.

Aziz, the local bread maker.

November 2004 in Khost, Afghanistan

CHAPTER 7

Welcome Home

"The world breaks everyone, and afterward,
some are strong at the broken places."
Ernest Hemingway

Coming home from war is surreal. Citizens have a preconceived notion as to what goes on "over there." Sadly, however, those notions are often based more on the latest Hollywood blockbuster than reality. People treat you in accordance with their inaccurate beliefs as to what occurs during deployments. At this time, most everyone in the country still conveys a great deal of support for our efforts overseas. Everyone back home seems so proud of me, yet I don't feel like I have done anything. Sure, there was a couple of small exchanges, but I was expecting *Black Hawk Down* level action. I think that's what the majority of people who know me believe I've been through.

Friends speak to me differently now and men who I looked up to growing up in the fire station give me a great deal more respect. I feel honored by the experience, but I also felt like a bit of a liar. I'm no war hero; I'm just happy to be home.

While home on leave, I tell my dad I need him to teach me how to drive a motorcycle. He recently purchased a brand-new Harley Davidson Road King, but still has his older Honda. He has a blast watching me struggle with the clutch in a parking lot near our house. We spend a couple of quality hours laughing at my lack of coordination. There's so many things I've never done, so many places I haven't been. Returning from deployment opens my eyes to that. I want to experience all of life. I want to see it all, touch it, smell it, and embrace all of what life has to offer. When we get home, I tell my dad, "We should go to Vegas!"

"What?"

"Yeah Dad, you and me should take the motorcycles to Vegas after your next shift!"

"You don't know how to ride a motorcycle."

"The fuck I don't, you just taught me."

I know Bruce won't turn down such a request from me, especially since I just returned from a war zone. I've never been to Vegas and I want to check the box in an epic way. When Jess and I were freezing our stones off during RIP, we talked about all the places we've been. I told him I consumed a beer in seven different states, a fact I was proud of at the time. I made a short list and decided I want to take a run at the entire country. I set a goal to drink a beer in every state during my four-year enlistment. Nevada will be next.

My pops agrees so long as I get my permit while he's at work the following day. We will go when he gets home from work. Of course I stay out until four in the morning, catching up with my friends the night prior. It doesn't matter. I'm in the garage packing the saddlebags at eight thirty when he arrives home from the fire station. He asks me what I'm doing as if we never talked about a seven-hour motorcycle ride to Sin City.

"Well," I inform him. "We're fucking going to Vegas!" I pull out my permit and shoot him a crooked grin. I don't believe my dad's ever been surprised by any of the shit I've pulled, but he has a new look on his face this morning for sure. He's a champ about the situation. He just walks in the house, changes into a pair of blue jeans, has a cup of coffee, and calls my stepmother to let her know he'll be in Vegas for the next three days. They waited until I returned home from Afghanistan to have their wedding, so they've been married for less than a week, and he's taking off with me to hit the Strip.

As we accelerate to over sixty miles per hour, I begin to regret my decision.

I've never been out of a parking lot on two wheels. Here we are on a desert highway with transport trucks buzzing past us. I've never clenched onto anything as hard as I death-grip the handlebars, but we make it. We make it every bit of those two hundred and seventy-five miles without a single stall; I don't dump the bike once, and when we arrive, the ear-to-ear grin on my dad's face makes the terrifying journey completely worth it. It's that moment I think most dads wait for, the time when your son also gets to be your best friend, when you get to do cool shit with him and not just be his parent.

In Vegas, he teaches me how to play poker, and wouldn't you know it, I pull off a royal flush playing a buck and a quarter a hand. The jackpot is still over $1,400. I'm unaware of the rule, but my father informs me that if you hit a hand like that you're obligated to pay for drinks for the rest of the trip. I'm happy to oblige after all he's done for me. It's three of the most fun days I can remember, sans the hung-over ride back through the desert.

Before I know it, my two weeks of leave is up and it's time to head back to Battalion. This will be my first full training cycle where I finally learn all of the cool trade secrets on how to kill a dozen men with my bare hands, shoot laser beams from my eyes, and all of the other hype.

CHAPTER 8

Away We Go

"War has no operating hours, no customer service department,
and sells the same product in 1000 different packages."
- Bryce Mahoney

There's nothing glamorous about the day-to-day life of a Ranger medic. The aggressive tones of the alarm clock snap me awake at four forty-five in the morning. I stumble through the dorm-style barracks room and into the joint kitchen area I share with another Ranger. Five minutes to hit the three S's (shit, shower, shave) and out the door. It's a five-minute walk from the barracks to the company area which is divided into the front offices and the back warehouse commonly referred to as "The Zoo." The Zoo is a dismal work environment, void of windows or fresh air. Most of the men below the rank of Sergeant First Class enter using the back entrance, passing the supply room manned by Brian Allen. Soldiers give the supply guy a lot of shit; I've never understood why. To me the supply Sergeant is the best guy to have on your side.

Giant wall lockers divide the three infantry platoons from one another, establishing Gangland-esque boundaries. As a private, entering into the wrong area could easily result in a phenomenon known as "getting balled up," which essentially means being tied into a pretzel by an overwhelming force of Rangers from rival sections of the same company.

Down the hall from the supply room and just before the aid station is a large closet dedicated to NBC (Nuclear Biological Chemical). Ranger Garza is the company's NBC expert who gets to spend a significant portion of his day sitting in said closet, a job he assures me sounded a lot cooler when his recruiter was pitching it to him. Just past the aid station is the arms room. The arms room is typically staffed by guys too injured to endure the rigorous day-to-day training. It's an opportunity for them to mend and still maintain an active role in the Ranger mission. One of the men working here has an impressive scar across his throat from an emergency cricothyroidotomy courtesy one of my fellow medics. A little farther down is a communications shop or "comms room" where the company radio equipment is maintained. The comms room is run by the heavily tattooed Sergeant Patterson. Patterson came up in the east coast hardcore punk scene where he played drums for the popular band The Hope Conspiracy. We became friends shortly after he discovered the drum kit in my barracks room. Past the comms room is the entrance to the front offices. This area is a serious danger zone for all new guys. All of the company's officers and senior enlisted men work here. Heaven forbid you have to enter that lion's den for any reason and are not completely squared away. A boot lace out of place or a random piece of thread protruding from your uniform is grounds for an impromptu workout.

Luckily for me, the aid station is where I spend most of my time pretending to be productive. It's cramped and often overcrowded with men looking for a reprieve from the monotony of cleaning weapons and doing push-ups. I'm one of Charlie company's seven medics. Six platoon medics work under Dano; me, Smith, Schramm, Robbins, Nicholson, and Lewis (not of the famed Lewis Lewis; incidentally, he works next door in Bravo Company). I'm acquainted with Nicholson, Lewis, and Dano from my first deployment, but I'm still getting to know the other guys. I like Robbins right away. He's an intelligent guy with a big smile, and the relationship he has with his men is second to none. His bedside manner and compassion are qualities I strive hard to emulate.

The aid station doors open before five in the morning. We don't have to wait long for our first customers to pile in. On any given day we have three to six patients with various complaints. Ailments range from minor aches and pains, to knife wounds from late night altercations, to penile irritation courtesy of the unsavory ladies of downtown Columbus. Any medical issues outside of our scope of practice are escorted across the street to the Battalion Aid Station (BAS). The BAS employs a handful of headquarter medics, a Physician's Assistant, and a surgeon. It features a fully stocked pharmacy and multiple treatment rooms. There's not much we can't treat in-house.

Shortly after sick call, the entire company does physical training, or "PT" for short. Most of the time I'm trusted to conduct my own workout, but every once in a while someone acts stupid at a bar and we all take the punishment for it. After PT we eat breakfast and get ready for whatever training is scheduled for the day. We drill all the time. Airborne operations, demolition practice, rifle time, medical training, and then some. A fifteen-hour day is common. We train, and train, and train some more. Between the constant deployments and this type of a day-to-day grind in the States, I have no clue how guys manage to stay married. I have so much respect for Ranger families; they're put through the grind right along with us. I don't know how some of the guys manage to balance a wife and children through all of it.

It took the better part of my first deployment to gain the trust of the men in third platoon. Within a week of returning to the U.S., however, I'm reassigned to second platoon where I have to prove myself once again. Smith's time in service is up. Robbins is the remaining platoon medic, and next in line for a Ranger school spot. Since our respective platoons were stationed in different parts of Afghanistan, the men in second platoon have no exposure to me. As a result, they believe I'm a brand new guy, despite coming up on two years in the Army. I'm treated accordingly. By the end of my first week with the new platoon, I'm convinced my name is "Hey You!" Each platoon in Ranger Battalion has their own unique personality. I'd grown comfortable with third platoon's laid-back demeanor, but things are different in second. Second platoon, or 2C, is more stoic, with a propensity for beating morale into their men.

In the middle of the training cycle, I jump at the opportunity to attend a medical course known as Operational Emergency Medical School (OEMS) in

Tacoma, Washington. It's a chance to cross train with Air Force Pararescuemen (PJ), Rangers from other Battalions, and SEAL Corpsmen. Also in attendance are a few corpsmen from the regular Navy. Training with other Special Operations medics from various units is normal, but I've had little interaction with conventional forces since going through RIP a few years earlier. I've grown to expect a certain level of experience and knowledge from guys we go to schools with. It's interesting seeing how conventional forces respond to the amount of advanced information provided at this particular course.

Following our initial orientation meeting, a small group of guys all inquire about any gym nearby. The closest one is a few miles away. Me, another Ranger medic, a SEAL Corpsmen and a PJ named Rob carpool to the facility. It's supposed to be a light day for me. The SEAL in our group lets us know, "I'm gonna do a mile warm up on the treadmill."

I didn't plan on running today, but I chime in, "Yeah that sounds like a good call." I look down to see what his speed is set to and match it. This begins the silent bidding war. He raises a notch, I raise two. He matches, I go faster. By the end of what is supposed to be a warm up run, we are both averaging well below a five-minute mile. Determined to not show fatigue, I proceed directly to the free weight section of the gym. My new friend Rob joins us by the dumbbells and for the next two and a half hours the three of us proceed to do just a little bit more than the previous guy, upping the ante. We're all exceptionally fortunate there's no Marine in our group, or we would still be there to this day, refusing to let our branch be the first to say when. The other Ranger, unburdened with the responsibility of representing the Regiment, demands we stop and go get something to eat.

We all do one final set of pull-ups and carry our tattered bodies to a nearby sushi restaurant where we once again get into a pissing contest. We start off with two rolls each and a beer, until one in the group orders a glass of sake. My hands are tied. I have to order as much or more of the potent rice wine. Wave upon endless wave of sushi rolls arrive at our table. The bill for the restaurant, which closed two hours ago, is over a hundred dollars each. A small price to pay to not come in second to a SEAL or PJ.

Even by Special Operation Forces (SOF) standards, the course is exceptionally progressive. We conduct a hypovolemia lab. The goal is to simulate the physiological event of losing a majority of the blood in your body. In order to mimic blood loss without actually losing any blood, test subjects (me) take a drug called Lasix, also known as the water pill. This drug encourages urination. I then put on a pair of inflatable pants that push all of the blood to my upper body. I also take a significant amount of a vasodilator under the tongue to open all of the blood vessels. I'm instructed to stand up as the pants are deflated. Since all of the blood vessels are wide open, the limited volume of fluid in my system drops away from the organs and into the legs. When they check my blood pressure, it's almost undetectable.

I successfully simulate the loss of about half the blood in my body. The doctor asks a series of questions including my name, rank, and social security number. I answer without hesitation. He instructs me to complete a couple of squats, again, no issues whatsoever. The good doctor then delivers the moral of the story. An incredibly fit Ranger or SEAL in his early twenties is going to compensate right up until the point where he dies. A guy who's been shot and lost half the blood in his body will still be ready to fight. As a Special Operations Medic, it's a valuable lesson which must always be kept in mind.

In addition to the shock lab, we practice nerve blocks on one another, learn advanced surgical techniques for field operations, and start intraosseous infusion on each other. Getting a Fast1 is like getting punched in the chest with half a dozen needles. Actually, getting a Fast1 IS getting punched in the chest with a half dozen needles. The primary needle punctures the sternum so fluid can be delivered directly into the bone. This is necessary if a patient lost so much blood that getting an IV started on the vein is not possible.

After class each day we sit in the hotel bar for happy hour. One afternoon the tall, slender brunette behind the bar asks my PJ friend Rob how he got the scar on his jaw. He replies, "I got shot in the neck." She laughs awkwardly the way a civilian does at a joke like that. "No, seriously, I got shot in the neck and it came out my face." He shows the equally impressive entrance wound and tells her about the mission in Afghanistan.

"That sounds like a book I just read called *None Braver*," I chime in.

"Yeah, that's me, Rob Disney."

"Get the fuck outta here."

"Bro, we've been hanging out all week and you didn't put those two things together?"

"So then, you're Rob Disney. That's pretty fucking badass." None of the other Rangers at the bar have any clue why I'm impressed. Rob and I have an impromptu jam session in the bar later in the week with an old guitar and a pair of drumsticks I brought with me.

The two-week course concludes with another live tissue lab which is significantly more comprehensive than the one we conducted at SOMC. We are some of the first people to try out a new intraosseous injection technology intended to be used with a small drill. The device looks like a giant thumb tack. I leave the drill on the table and pop the device directly into the patient's bone by hand. The representative for the company says she's never seen anyone use the device without the drill. "Yeah, well, I'm not about to add the weight of that useless piece of shit to my aid bag. Not if I can just corkscrew the little fucker in there." It's apparent she's accustomed to working with surgeons who may not be so quick with the expletives, but she appreciates the feedback. I take three of the prototype models for my aid bag, which collectively take up less space than a single Fast1.

During the trauma lane portion of the course I realize my patient needs a surgical airway and I don't have a scalpel. I use a boot knife to create a thumb size hole to slide the endotracheal tube in. When my patient shows signs of shock, I take out the emergency blanket in my aid bag and cuddle up its blood soaked body. I may not have outright won the gym session, or the sushi eat-off, but my patient stays alive longer than any other today. I get teased later that she's likely not the first or last pig I cuddle up with.

By the end of the first training cycle, I have a good grasp on things. I've gained the trust of my new platoon over six months of extensive training. I know who to avoid, and how much work needs to be done in a day. The training cycle culminates in a final event known as platoon evaluations. A Ranger platoon has a lot of moving parts; this is the time their synchronicity is tested over several stressful days. First platoon's medic performs below the standard for Ranger Battalion. As a result, he's reassigned to another unit, leaving the platoon without a medic. Dano makes the choice to transfer me once again. It's bittersweet. For the third time in under a year I'm the new guy and am forced to earn the men's trust. The upside is I will now be a senior platoon medic. The transfer impacts Robbins as well. With me leaving, his Ranger school spot is pulled. There will be no one to provide medical care for second platoon while he's gone. We are as lean on medics as a Ranger company can be and still operate.

I move out of the barracks and in with my friend, Matt. By now Matt is in charge of the medics who graduate RIP and are awaiting SOMC spots. He's one of the few to take on Ranger school and be deployed prior to SOMC, making him an obvious choice for an early leadership position within Regiment. The scar on the back of his head is still very visible from our Panama City outing a year and a half earlier.

CQB training on Ft. Benning, Georgia.

CHAPTER 9

Here to Mars

"The difficulty is not so great to die for a friend,
as to find a friend worth dying for."
Homer

"Should we have a BBQ for the fourth of July this weekend?" Matt asks as we sit around our townhouse playing beer pong with shots of whiskey.

"This is America, isn't it?" I respond before having to take yet another shot. His accuracy is prodigious.

It's late June, 2005, and I'm preparing to leave on my second combat deployment. Matt and I share a two-story, three-bedroom condo considered "on-post" housing on Fort Benning. Just as Matt and I begin planning our "Happy Birthday America" debauchery, I receive a page from my company to return immediately. This means one of two things. Either some moron was caught doing something illegal and our entire company has to pee in a little plastic cup, or we're getting a high-profile mission, which will require us to be wheels up very soon.

As always, deployment bags are already packed and staged in the Zoo. Most of the guys live within the brown fence of our compound, so by the time I arrive there's already a shitstorm of chaos. Rangers frantically look for various pieces of mission-essential equipment and speculate as to what's going on. I know better than to ask my new platoon sergeant what's happening. Even though he and I were both serendipitously assigned to first platoon, we already have a history together.

Now, Sergeant First Class Strait is one of the cadre responsible for, well, let's say "motivating" my class during RIP. Seeing his figure moving down the hall still makes my bones cold, reminiscent of the long evenings at Cole Range. So I have plenty of reasons to keep my distance. He's not a huge man, but you can't tell by looking at his eyes. There is an intensity in them, that quiet intensity of a man who will not hesitate to punch you in the face.

By nightfall, my platoon walks through the humid Georgia night to board a cargo plane on what feels like an abandoned runway. I'm still not entirely sure what's going on. I get to be the popular guy during this long flight. It's my job to hand out Ambien to anyone not interested in being awake for the eighteen-hour journey on the noisy military cargo plane. I pass the little white pills out like Skittles on Halloween.

There's several reasons these flights are uncomfortable. First of all, the seats are just cargo nets. We're allowed to lay on the metal floor once the plane hits a certain altitude, but laying on cold steel for the better part of a day isn't exactly soothing. Most guys opt out by taking the popular sleeping pill and go black for several hours. The next thing I remember is landing in Germany to refuel, still groggy from the double dose of the happy little pill.

The second leg of the flight is far less restful as I begin to receive information on what we're doing. Apparently there's a group of Navy SEALs who were compromised in a remote province of Afghanistan and we're going in as part of a combat search and rescue team (CSAR).

I know what you are thinking; I was thinking the exact same thing. *Why wouldn't they deploy a team already in Afghanistan?* They did. This became the next point of my great unrest. The Chinook helicopter containing eight members of the 160th Special Operations Aviation Regiment (SOAR) and eight U.S. Navy SEALs was shot down en route to aid the compromised members of SEAL Team 10 as a Quick Reaction Force (QRF). All of those men lost their lives coming to the aid of their brothers.

Upon landing at Bagram Air Field (BAF), we have just enough time to grab ammo and MREs and meet at the airfield. My stomach sinks as I find out our Chinook will be following the identical flight path of the one recently shot down. We sit on the airfield waiting for darkness to fall over the distant mountains which will soon become the proving ground for our young platoon.

While we wait, we see a group of A-10 pilots getting ready to take off. As if they knew exactly where we were about to go, they give us a strong thumbs up from the cockpit. Members from each of the different branches of the military love to give each other a hard time, but when it comes down to it, there's a very deep level of respect for the job the others do. We don't realize it now, but these men will be our salvation once we hit the ground. It's evident by the gesture they give us from their cockpit they have a great deal of respect for the job we're about to do as well.

Story of the Year speaks directly to me through the tiny headphones buried into my ears. "Anthem of Our Dying Day" rings out in crisp synchronicity with the moment. "Just a ghost to the world." The snare drum pop, pop, pop, pops in perfect time with the belt-fed weapon to my left, laying cover fire on the tree tops below.

Searing serenity, I accept death. I embrace the stink of his foul breath in this moment. I'm already dead. I look to the stoic, shadowed ghost faces of the men around me, each accepting demise in their own way, welcoming the immortality which accompanies death. Each pair of cold eyes fixate on the ramp leading to war's abyss. The night swallows us, one by one, as we exit the back of the hovering Chinook helicopter. I can make out the outline of each one of the other Rangers who, without instruction, form a semi-circle formation.

We face out and pull security as the bird pulls away and disappears into the night. And in an instant, we sit in eerie silence. The stars are in abundance like I've never before seen. A billion lives being lived light years away, unconcerned by our peril. Surrounded by a platoon of Rangers, I feel perfectly alone. Stranded now, somewhere between nowhere and nothing. The air is cold and thin as it passes with labor into my lungs. One at a time, we pick up and move to a rally point. I can feel the effects of the high altitude stealing my breath.

To my surprise, we see a group of men sitting around a campfire. Like us, they don't have any unit identifying patches. They look like a small contingent of Special Forces guys, but could be SEALs. I don't ask. I'm surprised by the campfire. It doesn't seem like an operationally sound decision to me, but this is my first time in these mountains.

Even as we set up a patrol base, I'm still not entirely sure what's going on. I spent most of my first year as a Ranger having almost no clue as to what's actually happening. At a company level the First Sergeant delegates to his platoon sergeants, those platoon sergeants pass the information to their squad leaders, the squad leaders pass the info to their team leaders who pass it to their privates. *Let the medic know what the fuck is going on* isn't really in that chain. Most of the time I pester one of my buddies who's a team leader to let me know what we're doing.

One of the new guys begins to complain of a severe headache, which worries me. It may be altitude sickness. Just forty-eight hours ago we were sitting at sea level, and if I was cool enough to have one of those sweet GPS watches like the other guys, I could tell you we're now sitting at nearly 10,000 ft. Even if someone did get altitude sickness there's not much I can do about it. The treatment calls for a drug called Mannitol, in a dose that would be way too much to carry with me. It's a risk we're taking.

The first night is quiet, but no one sleeps. The entire platoon understands the importance of this mission. As the sun rises, it exposes the most beautiful country my eyes have ever seen. It's the most expansive, remote, and wild terrain imaginable. Even now in early July, when the midday highs reach over a hundred degrees, there remains snow-capped mountains in the distance. Between those peaks and our patrol base, countless towering coniferous trees scrape the edge of the sky.

My gazing session is short-lived. The sun is up and it's time to begin our first patrol. My inexperience is evident as I realize having both an aid bag and an assault pack will make navigating this terrain miserable. *Why did I bring two separate bags?* I use a carabiner to snap the two together. Within the first forty meters of our movement I realize how awful this will truly be. The assault pack is sitting on top of my aid bag and every step causes it to swing around to the side and smack me in the head.

I've always said, *if you're going to be dumb you better be tough.* I'm stupid for not packing more effectively and receive a reminder of my error with every step.

We traverse some of the gnarliest terrain my feet have ever experienced. The slopes become so severe, it is necessary to place a hand on the ground. We shift from a wedge type formation into a snake-like single file. I'm the third to last person in the movement. The guy behind me is an Air Force Combat Controller. The guy behind him is an Afghan Special Forces member known as a "Mohawk."

I ask them both if they get the feeling we're being followed. They both have the same intuitive reaction. I hear footsteps behind us. We're being hunted. My skin vibrates in one of the most uncomfortable sensations I've ever experienced. This is my first mission as Sergeant First Class Strait's medic. I suppress the memories of low crawling through a partially frozen mud puddle to relay the information. Thirty seconds later I hear shots ring out, *POP . . . POP, POP, POP,* echoing off the surrounding mountains.

"Enemy target, two hundred meters to the right!" announces Sergeant Guell, one of the platoon's squad leaders.

Every weapon system in the platoon orients in that direction. As the platoon sergeant spins to get eyes on the target, he loses his footing. He slides thirty feet down the steep terrain and is finally stopped by a stump. Knowing he isn't hurt, my first thought is, *that's what you get for making me crawl in that fucking ice pond!* I know what you're thinking, I'm an asshole. Well, you're right. I am an asshole. That thought is immediately followed by the instinct to run in the direction of the enemy.

I take off in a hard sprint up the hill and to the right of our platoon. I drop behind a cluster of rocks that provide decent cover for the firefight about to take place. My platoon sergeant makes his way up the mountainside and settles in next to my location. I ask him if he is alright. He nods quickly and our focus shifts to the Taliban versus Ranger firefight about to go down.

Nothing. Nothing happens. A few quick shots from one our guys and then nothing. It's like having a random girl at a bar grab your junk then just leave. Now here I am left with a combat chub and nothing to shoot at. Within a few minutes we pick up and continue our movement, at times having to literally crawl on our hands and knees in certain areas.

My good friend Josh, who has the appropriate nickname "the angry leprechaun," has the unfortunate task of hauling the ammo for the 240B. A 240B is a belt-fed weapon that dispenses 7.62 rounds like confetti at a parade. Josh is a stud; he wrestled in college and carries an "I'd rather die than give up" attitude, which is a common theme among successful Rangers. The combination of the altitude, heat, and sixty plus pounds of gear will wear on anyone, however, and he's no exception. I can tell he's getting his lunch money taken and ask him if he wants an I.V. He refuses so I give him a packet of Gatorade and sit with him for a moment. He recovers quickly and we continue to crawl up the side of the steep mountain for the next half hour. This makes me much more aware of how the men are responding to these rigors. I feel okay, but I've spent a decent amount of time in my youth hunting in the mountains of Northern Arizona. My father and I used to cover thirty plus miles in a weekend hunt across demanding terrain. And while this makes Arizona hiking feel like walking from Cinnabon down to the Hot Topic at the mall, it's still a better introduction than my friend from Iowa ever received growing up.

As the sun sets on our first day in the Kunar, we set up our patrol base. Do you remember that kid in school who asked, "When are we ever going to use this? Why do we have to learn this?"

Well, that kid was me in basic training when we went over how to set up a Claymore mine. A Claymore is a directional, anti-personnel mine which was used frequently in Vietnam, but has become a relic of sorts by modern warfare standards. Right up there with the bayonet. So needless to say, when my platoon sergeant gives the order for us to set them up just outside of the patrol base I'm taken aback. *It's 2005 and we're Rangers! Don't we have something a little more high speed than a fucking Claymore?* Lucky for me, the instructions "Front toward enemy" are idiot proof. (Sorry Matt, I know that's why you got No-Go'ed in Ranger school.)

With our cool guy booby traps in place and the first watch posted up, I decide to check on each of the guys. I walk around checking feet for blisters, handing out pieces of candy from my "morale pouch," and making sure no one sustained any injuries throughout the day. Some time during the night we get a care package in the form of a one-ton pallet dropped from a C-130 cargo plane full of water, medical supplies, food, and batteries. I gather up several I.V. bags and pre-package them with everything necessary to get a line started. I make four of these and give one to each of the squad leaders. One of them complains about having to carry the weight. I explain to him that I already have six of them in my bag, plus every bit of equipment he's carrying.

The next morning I find the blue package hidden in the bush where he was laying the night before. What a shithead. I pick up the bag and add it to the contents of my pack. My platoon sergeant calls me over. "We need to set up a choke point, Doc." I'm at a complete loss. I have no idea what he's talking about. I think maybe it could be another Vietnam-era Ranger trap. I feel pretty dumb when he just wants me to take a knee and count the Rangers walking out of the patrol base to make sure we have everyone.

It's midday and we've been walking for hours. The temperature on my buddy's cool-guy watch says 102. We find the set of huts we suspect is the home of some of the Taliban members involved in the firefight. We find a decent spot to set up overwatch and a team goes into the house. It's more of a shack really. It has dirt floors and only three walls made of sticks and mud. There's a fireplace and a couple of utensils. There's a section of the hut designated for chickens. This guy definitely wins the award for lowest carbon footprint. I will say this, the view more than makes up for his lack of appliances. It's breathtaking. I can see terraces across the ravine and mountains in the distance covered in snow. What's the old saying? *I'd rather live in a shack and stare at a castle than live in a castle and stare at a shack.* No one's home, well besides the chickens. We do a quick search and find nothing. As we're searching a nearby ravine I hear a call come over the radio.

"There's monkeys."

"Repeat last."

"Ummmm, there's a pack of big ass baboons staring at us. And so help me God if they get any closer I am going to open up on them with the 240!"

It was Josh and Arter on overwatch. Now I know what you're thinking,

"There aren't any baboons in Afghanistan." Well listen here: there are! There are a dozen Rangers who will confirm it. It's a pack of huge, fang-toothed baboons!

We keep our distance and patrol the area in small teams looking for any signs of a firefight. One of the patrol teams finds several 5.56 shell casings so we know this is where shit went down, but there's no sign of the SEALs.

Four guys with very impressive beards, wearing shorts walk up to our overwatch position. They're members of a SEAL team. My first thought is, look at these shit-bags wearing shorts. Then I realize it's over a hundred degrees out and wearing shorts would be amazing right now. *Wait, why the fuck are we wearing pants? And long sleeve DCU tops? Damn, I should've gone to BUDs.* We exchange information. They tell us they have Intel that one of the local goat herders has information on one of the missing SEALs.

We move out to the houses in the valley below. A couple of our guys accompany the SEALs while I and the other half of our platoon pull security. They find out the body of one of the guys we're searching for is nearby. One of the locals agrees to show us where he is, for a price. I'm not sure how much they give the man, but I imagine it's difficult for them to not pay him with a punch to his opportunistic throat.

We recover the body of Matt Axelson, a Navy SEAL from California who turned twenty-nine just three days prior. They anticipate the moment; one of the SEALs pulls out a black body bag. Throughout my time in the military I've been exposed to countless acts of absolute professionalism, but this moment ranks among the top. The four men refuse our help. They will carry their brother out themselves, a decision I hold in the highest regard.

It's starting to get late and we begin to move away from the shacks. We set up another patrol base and call for an additional resupply drop. This one doesn't come quite as close as the last one. It impacts the side of the mountain with the force of a Mack truck striking a Jetta on the freeway. The pallet explodes, which really wouldn't be an issue if it didn't impact on a portion of the mountain featuring a twenty percent grade. This causes a diarrhea-like explosion of water bottles and MREs, scattering our supplies all the way down the mountainside.

By this point, we're fatigued and severely dehydrated. The thought of having to climb down the mountain to recover our water is heartbreaking. A team is assigned to do the recovery. There's a couple of body bags in the supply drop. We use one of them to carry our food and water back up the mountain to our patrol base. We're able to recover about half a bag's worth for our entire platoon. It's spread thin among the guys.

Back in the patrol base I begin checking feet and general morale. My platoon sergeant's feet are wet. I dig into my bag and pull out a small container of foot powder and a fresh pair of socks. He tilts his head a little and says, "Squared away, Doc!" It's the first compliment I receive from him. It's a subtle statement, but raises my spirits and makes me feel ten feet tall.

As the sun begins to set I find a cozy little spot under a bush in hopes of finally getting some sleep. The magnetic weight of my heavy eyelids draws them closed. I'm asleep for maybe an hour when I'm snapped awake by the sound of an A-10 Thunderbolt "fast mover" dropping hate on targets via some big ass American bombs. It's the same pilots who gave us the thumbs up as we waited to board the Chinook. They're looking out for us, our guardian angels no doubt.

The first explosion is so close! My eyes rip open, my brain tells my hand to reach for my rifle, but my body refuses to respond. I'm paralyzed with fear. I literally can't move. My pants are wet. *Did I piss myself?* As my hyperventilating subsides, I'm finally able to turn my head. I look around to see the rest of my platoon in a hyper-vigilant state. I take a knee and give my pants the sniff test. *It's not urine, that's good.* It started to rain a little while I was asleep. The bomb runs done by the A-10s continue throughout the night. It's called a show of force. And if I'm this startled, I'm sure those Taliban assholes are shitting themselves.

I'm unable to sleep the rest of the night. By daybreak I take three extra guard shifts so the guys could get a little more sleep. Being up all night allows me the opportunity to see another picturesque sunrise. It's possible the rising sun appears so spectacular due to the vast, untouched countryside it spills itself over, but it's been my experience no sunrise ever looks as good as the one ascending after a night filled with near-death experiences. It's possible the sun rises in such a glorious spectrum of color and sanguinity every morning, we just see that hope more clearly after it's nearly taken from us forever.

The morning light means it's time to move. My platoon sergeant and I set up another choke point to count everyone off. This time I know what it means. I'm becoming a pro at counting to thirty-eight. So far, the terrain we've experienced is the most austere I've ever traversed, and it's about to get even worse.

Within an hour, the world just drops off. We find ourselves descending down five hundred meters of loose slate rock on an unbelievably steep grade. I'm still not sure how the SEALs could have conducted a firefight in this environment. The layered rock frequently breaks under the weight of the Ranger's feet, sending large sharp rocks tumbling past the men below. It's incredible no one is seriously injured during the movement. In addition to the danger of the falling rocks, we're incredibly exposed. If the enemy set up in the right position, they'd be able to take out our entire platoon with a single machine gun.

When we reach the bottom of the cliff we arrive at the village we've been searching for. Chills shoot down my spine when we find shards of American uniforms on the ground just outside the village. The bloody pieces of camouflage clothing strewn about so closely resemble the ones covering my body. A startling reminder of how real the situation is. This isn't a training exercise. No one is carrying blanks and no one will be calling endex at the end.

We need to speak to the village elder. It's our best hope of gaining information. Our platoon leader sets out with a couple of guys to find him. The rest of us take up security positions around the village. Something seems out of place. My platoon sergeant and I both notice a well-dressed man. His shifty, beady eyes give him away first. It's impossible to hide true hate; it shines right through your eyes and onto the world. He's far too well-kept to be a goat herder. His crisp, clean, white tunic contrasts the general appearance of every other member of the village. His sparkling gold watch is not something a goat herder would wear.

The rest of the villagers are in old, tattered garments with dirty, snarled hair and beards. They resemble how I imagine the characters of the Bible to appear. Trapped in some sort of mountainous time capsule, preserved from the rest of the world for two thousand years. We keep an eye on the out-of-place man, but can't do anything about him. We're in no position to start slinging accusations. We're guests here and clearly out numbered. We're in their village attempting to get information that will hopefully lead to the recovery of our brothers-in-arms; harassing one of the locals will easily shut down their hospitality, so he gets a pass.

We get little information from the village elder. The guys who conduct the interview tell me he's apprehensive about giving any information, and that he seems scared. This is common in Afghanistan. The vast majority of the people are simple, hard-working farmers and herders. They're bullied and intimidated by a select few whose contorted interpretation of a religious ideology has left them in the crossfire.

As we leave the village we're notified we'll soon be extracted. We need to move roughly nine kilometers to our exfil point. Typically, that isn't enough of a distance to make any one of us break a sweat. However, at this point almost everyone is severely dehydrated and without water. It's over a hundred degrees and this is some of the nastiest country in the world.

We'll be extracted just past dark, so it only gives us a short time to get to our grid coordinate. Most of the platoon hides their discomfort well up until this point. Those nine kilometers become the breaking point, though. Guys start to really fall apart. Most of us have had less than four hours of sleep in the past four days. Add in the acclimatization to high altitude and lack of water, and we're getting close to being combat ineffective.

I start an I.V. on the Radio Telephone Operator (RTO). His eyes roll to the back of his head. He is tachycardic and his skin is hot and dry. He has literally sweated out everything in his system. His body no longer has the ability to cool itself and his temperature is increasing rapidly. He's carrying the AN/PRC-117F radio. With the extra batteries, the radio adds over twenty more pounds to his pack. I become concerned for the rest of the men, knowing our RTO is a pretty tough guy. I remember back to the lessons learned at OEMS about Rangers being able to compensate right up to the point of death. With these symptoms, it won't be long before we're having to carry some of them out, placing an even greater strain on those remaining.

Putting one guy and all of his equipment into a litter places a massive burden on the rest of the platoon and in this environment is almost guaranteed to create a domino effect. If he's this bad off, it's only a matter of time before more guys start going down.

I quickly make my way up to the front of the file formation. Once I get to the front I stop and face the men as they walk past me. I attempt to see how well they're focusing and if anyone is stumbling or showing any other signs of distress. The thing about Rangers, and most members of Special Operations, is they rarely tell you they're hurt. They pride themselves on their ability to endure incredible amounts of suffering. So I have to be a little tricky and observe them as they walk by. When the very last man reaches me I repeat the process, running back to the front of the formation in an effort to look into each pair of sunken eyes. I do this at least three more times before reaching our exfil point. One of the guys on his first deployment is sitting, head down, when I approach him. He's displaying all of the same symptoms as our RTO.

"Hey, Brandon, are you alright bud?"

"Yeah, Doc, I'm just a little out of breath."

"What's the matter, you're not used to walking for three days at 10,000 feet in hundred-degree weather without water?"

"Ha, no, Doc, I guess I'm not."

"Well, you look good. I mean that, you're a good-looking man!"

Brandon just smiles and shakes his head. We need to get moving. I have a small packet of Gatorade at the bottom of my pack. I take it out and mix it with the last eight ounces of hot water I have left. "Drink this." After another couple of minutes Brandon stands up. Not the way a six-foot, two-hundred-pound Ranger usually stands, it's more like the way a fawn stands for the first time. I can see he doesn't have much left in him. I do the math in my head. With several more clicks to travel I decide carrying his thirty-five-pound assault pack will be a lot easier than attempting to drag his two-hundred-pound ass in a Skedco.

"Let me see your pack, bud."

His squad leader interjects. "No, I'll take it, Doc."

"Roger that, Sergeant."

I chuckle as I see the frustration mounting in the squad leader's face as the second pack bobbles and hits him in the side of the head. He makes a comment about how bad this sucks.

"Yeah, tell me about it, Sergeant. My second bag's been hitting me for the last three days." He looks at me in awe, as if his pack was the heaviest one on anyone's back this entire time. He doesn't complain again.

We're getting close now. The last two kilometers are a straight shot. We're moving uphill on an old dirt road. I move through the platoon and ask how guys are doing one more time. Arter projectile vomits without slowing down; he doesn't miss a single step. What a tough son of a bitch. He's been carrying that 240B this entire time. Without any ammo that belt-fed weapon weighs nearly thirty pounds. I have no idea how he managed up and down some of those rock faces with that massive, cumbersome weapon system. His squad leader tells Arter to give him the weapon. Arter refuses; he won't give up his weapon. Tough, prideful, impressive bastard. He vomits one more time without skipping a beat. My dehydrated heart swells with pride knowing that I'm in the same unit with men like this. We all put ourselves through a tortuous selection process, not for a special-colored hat or arm insignia, but for the honor and privilege of working alongside men like that; men who, in the most inhospitable environment, under the greatest stress imaginable, refuse to back down an inch. I know 100 percent in this moment he would give his life for me and I would do the same for him. This is why these men will forever be my brothers.

As we reach the Objective Rally Point (ORP), I see a few guys in digital cammies. It's a squad of Marines. I didn't expect to see that. We've felt so isolated for what seems like so long that seeing other US uniforms is almost startling. When we get to a cluster of trees and see several more men, a feeling of relief settles over me. Then I see some guy hanging out with his shirt off. There's a group of SEALs sitting around a radio. In all, a couple dozen Americans from different units are gathered here. It's amazing how isolated the little villages are from the rest of the world, surrounded by hundreds of miles of mountains that make the skyscrapers of our largest cities seem like insignificant toys.

Our first order of business when we reach the ORP is water. We ask a few of the men pulling security if they have any. One of the Marines tells us there's several cases remaining from a resupply drop down in the trees. What a relief. We dispatch a fire team to retrieve enough for the platoon. The bottles sat in the sun for days and are close to the temperature of the water in a tea kettle just before that obnoxious whistle starts. Just as I finish my first bottle, my platoon leader calls me over. "One of the guys is down." *Shit! Now? Really?*

It's one of the squad leaders. As I approach I begin my assessment by simply asking him what's going on. He blinks his eyes a couple of times in an attempt to focus on me the way a boxer does after he's had his bell rung.

"Hey, Doc," is all he says.

His breathing is short and shallow. He's lying propped up against a rock. As I begin to remove his boots, I tell him to take off his shirt and loosen his belt. His skin is hot and dry to the touch. I'm not surprised at this point. I pour some water on his neck in hopes it will quickly evaporate, helping his body to cool. I pull the blue bag containing the I.V. setup kit, the very same one which this very same squad leader discarded at our first patrol base. There's embarrassment in his eyes as I brandish the bag in front of him. He knows he fucked up; there's no point making a big deal about it. While asking him a series of questions, I start an I.V. on his right arm. By this point it's such a routine procedure I don't even think about it, I'm on autopilot. While giving my platoon leader a full assessment, he interrupts me and gives me the most off-hand compliment I've ever received. "Damn, Doc, cool under pressure. So cool maybe you should stick some of those water bottles up your ass to chill them down so we can actually drink them." It's the only situation in life I could consider having another man tell me to shove something up my ass as a compliment.

The bird arrives soon after. In the swirling dust and debris, we board the Chinook helicopter. I can't speak for the rest of the men, but it's one of the toughest helo rides of my Ranger carrier. We were dispatched to find four of our brothers, men we didn't know but knew all about. They may have been in a different branch, but they joined for the same reasons we did. They went through the same torture to earn the right to fight alongside the elite. They fought the same fight and bled the same blood. And here we are, departing in their time of need. I know that every other Ranger on that bird would have walked those mountains until their feet were bloody stumps to find those men. We never met them, but that doesn't mean we don't love them.

When we arrive back at Bagram Air Field we are greeted by our First Sergeant. He shakes each one of our hands and tells us good work. The ambivalence in my heart is overwhelming. We get back just in time for midrats, a meal the chow hall is open for between dinner and breakfast. Midnight rations is mainly for pilots and flight crews who keep odd hours. It's the best meal of the day because you can get breakfast and dinner together. There's something incredibly satisfying about getting waffles with your steak, especially when you haven't eaten more than a couple of MREs total in several days.

In the true fashion of the Ranger Regiment we're forced to shave, shower, and change into clean uniforms before being allowed to go eat. We end up missing the chow hall hours because of the order from a senior enlisted NCO and will have to wait until breakfast for a hot meal. After helping conduct what becomes one of the most significant search and rescue missions in the Global War on Terrorism, we wouldn't want to go to get our Froot Loops and lasagna looking dirty, now would we?

A man who sat and watched our three-day movement from an office, while sipping coffee, reprimands us the day after we get back to Bagram for not wearing our body armor during the search and rescue. We're told by that individual since we're not fit enough to fight in armor, we're required to start doing "combat PT" in addition to our normal workout routine. This involves going out in the middle of the day, in a full kit, in one hundred-plus degree heat, and running for over an hour at a time. This is put into effect within twenty-four hours of our return from our extended mission. Guys are severely dehydrated and likely close to a condition called rhabdomyolysis. Rhabdomyolysis is a product of severe muscle tissue breakdown compromising the ability of the kidneys to function.

I still haven't slept since we returned. The reality of those A-10s dropping bombs so close to us has not left me. As I lay in my bunk fighting the pain of exhaustion, one of the privates in my platoon runs into my tent and tells me something is wrong with one of our guys. There are no duty hours for a medic; your job is the men, always. When I get to him he's seizing on the gym floor. His core temperature is well over a hundred. He should have been resting after that mission, but instead he's engaging in a pointless act, handed down by a man trying to prove a point. Now he's at risk of permanent brain damage if the proper interventions aren't initiated.

I take Brandon to the aid station where we begin active cooling techniques. I deliver my assessment to the doctor on duty. He allows me to treat the patient myself as he sits back and asks me a few questions. By the time Brandon has a few liters of I.V. fluid on board, my platoon leader and platoon sergeant arrive. The doctor tells them the Ranger's condition and that I executed as a medic flawlessly.

This, in addition to my performance on the search and rescue mission we just concluded, is enough to get my platoon sergeant's attention. He tells me he's promoting me. Nothing could feel better. I'm going to be a Sergeant! My best friends, Matt and Jess, have already achieved the rank and now I'm joining them. I swell with pride and instantly grow two inches.

"Congrats, Doc, you just made Corporal."

What the fuck does that mean? I think to myself. No one gets a promotion to Corporal. I'm already an E4, how are you going to promote me to E4? All of the responsibility of a Sergeant without the respect or pay increase. Thanks again, Army, you sure do know your way around a practical joke! I will admit, having my platoon sergeant and platoon leader both recognize my competency and reward it with a pair of stripes means more to me than any medal I ever receive.

Waiting for nightfall to infill to the Kunar province.

Sunrise in the Kunar.

Seconds before shots are fired. Notice how steep the terrain is.
You can see four Rangers from my platoon if you look closely.

Inside the mountaintop home.

Antouine James Castaneda on overwatch.

Russell Tassin on overwatch. Just after the baboons rolled up.

Close to where we recovered Navy SEAL, Matt Axelson.

"I can't believe Marissa would treat Ryan that way, it's just cold-blooded."

"It's just not right, especially after all he's done for her!"

"What a bitch . . . should we watch another episode before midrats?"

"Does the Pope shit in the woods?"

We're a few weeks into this deployment and have already devolved into marathon sessions of *The O.C.* Our platoon hit the ground running when we assisted with the search and rescue operation for the Navy SEALs compromised during Operation Red Wings, but the operation tempo has come to a standstill. The summer of '05 is starting to feel like the winter of '04, sitting around Forward Operating Base Salerno.

This time I'm staying at Bagram Airfield, acting primarily as a Quick Reaction Force. That sounds cool, but what it really means is putting all of your kit on and sitting on the airfield for hours while another platoon is hitting an objective. So when the opportunity presents to jock up and walk in the mountains for a day or two, we jump. The new season of *The O.C.* isn't available in Afghanistan, and no one is willing to stoop to watching *Desperate Housewives* yet.

As I enter the room where the mission briefing is held, I see a very familiar bearded face. "Teddy P?" Ohh shit. I just referred to a Master Sergeant by his nickname. The last time I saw Teddy, we were students together at the Special Operations Medical Course at Ft. Bragg. I just pinned Corporal so addressing a Master Sergeant this way gets some abrasive looks from my superiors. Teddy works as a medic for a Civil Affairs unit and is putting together a MEDCAP mission (Medical Civil Action Program). The idea is to put a group of Americans into a village of tactical significance and supply medical supplies and treatment to its inhabitants.

It's an atypical mission for Rangers to conduct from my experience, but we really don't mind. Not just because the general boredom we're battling against, but because we view ourselves as consummate professionals. We don't see the difference between executing this task and hostage rescue mission or a search and rescue mission or a direct action raid. It's our job and it's time to go to work.

We load onto two Chinook helicopters piloted by the 160th SOAR. I'm not sure if there is another unit anywhere in the US military I've come to respect more than the Special Operations Aviation Regiment. Each night men from every unit in JSOC put their lives into the hands of those flight crews with absolute faith they will deliver them into and from harm's way. They are truly the unsung heroes of the US Special Operations community.

Tonight will do little to test their skill. We land in a rocky riverbed about five kilometers from the village and step from the ramp of the bird with motivation. As the helos pull away, the contrast of incessant violent vibration and dissonance of the dual rotor aircraft juxtaposed with the tranquility of the star-filled Afghan night is nearly maddening. The stars sparkle and shine like the first look into the eyes of a woman you've been estranged from for far too long. They greet us with a shimmer that can only exist in the vast expansiveness of this type of wild.

One by one we step off, creating a textbook Ranger file. The moon illuminates the outlines of the men in front and behind as we move from the low ground to the security of the terraces ahead. Ahead of me is our Battalion surgeon. We'll call him "Colonel O" since he still holds a position requiring anonymity. Col. O came to us from another unit in JSOC at the time of our deployment. I spoke with him a few times at the aid station on BAF, but most of the men have not met him. He's an incredibly intelligent man I find to be highly likeable. We also have a SEAL corpsman and a few other medics from Regiment with our platoon, including Sgt. Prokop. Prokop graduated Ranger school the week I first arrived at 3rd Ranger Battalion. He helped to square me away prior to my first deployment.

As we move through the night, I can tell the surgeon is struggling a bit. We take a tactical pause and I ask if he's doing alright. I'm not sure if he's accustomed to moving at a Ranger pace over this type of terrain. He makes some comment about the weight of his ruck and not realizing we'd be walking this far. I reach for his ruck, sitting at his side, nearly giving myself a hernia as I lift it. "Jesus, sir! You win the award for packing the most shit, that's for sure!"

I offer to take his pack for him, an offer he gladly accepts. Since our mission brief today occurred during my scheduled gym time, and I hate missing leg day, it's a win-win situation. Every one of the dozen or so terraces becomes a weighted muscle-up, which I find to be a fun little game. It takes another hour or so to reach the village. It's still dark so we'll have to sit and wait for first light to make contact with the village elder.

My platoon sergeant and I sit back to back against an old tree about thirty meters from one of the small mud houses. I slowly pull apart the Velcro strip keeping my shoulder pocket shut and retrieve a much-needed treat. Most Rangers would take the opportunity to pack their lip with chew, but I never took to that habit. Instead I pour the contents of the bright red bag into my hand. *Fuck, I love Skittles*, I think to myself as I fill my cheek like a chipmunk preparing for winter. The sweat accumulated from our march is creating quite the chill as we sit motionless in the tenebrous evening. This is how these things go. Hurry up and wait.

I'm curious about the time Sergeant First Class Strait spent as an instructor. I begin to inquire about some of the events during his time as a RIP cadre. I ask about certain guys who were kicked out and others who passed and how those things came to be. When I ask if he ever feels bad about any of his actions during that time he responds, "There was one time in a winter class that had a combination of sleet and snow during our time at Cole Range. I remember there being a giant puddle that the top sheet had frozen over on. We made those guys low crawl back and forth through that ice water all night long."

"Yeah, that was my class, Sergeant," I reply.

"I don't want to talk about this anymore!" he responds abruptly.

I want to ask him about his family, but I know he keeps those cards close to his chest. It's common here. It's not that guys don't want to talk about their family. It's something I don't understand being a single guy. Maybe it's just too painful, the missing, the absence. I imagine you have to turn off the loving husband and father part of yourself in order to be the other guy, the one who must embrace violence at any given moment. I don't pester him anymore.

As the sun stands up, it casts light to the beauty of our surroundings. The modest Afghan homes are dispersed sporadically against the backdrop of the steep mountains. Our Civil Affairs counterparts are making contact with the village elders as we display one of the skills Rangers are known the world over for . . . *take a knee, face out, pull security.* The news spreads quickly there's American doctors in the village handing out medicine. People start coming from every direction. It's a slightly uncomfortable scenario for many of us. We're not accustomed to being in a village during the day. We don't do presence patrols or spend much time with locals traditionally. The times we're on target past daybreak, we typically do everything we can to keep locals as far away as possible. We're being forced to adapt to the nature of the mission as fighting age men walk up to us. We're here to create a relationship, not start a fight.

A line starts to form outside of one of the larger homes. Within minutes every man, woman, and child from the entire village stands to receive treatment for some type of aliment. When asked, many don't know how old they are. They respond, "Between twenty and thirty." The Chinook is like a time machine. People well into their thirties have never seen a dentist or doctor, and it shows. I spend the first couple of hours cleaning out minor wounds. Injuries which have festered for some time. Imagine something as simple as stubbing your toe in a grocery store parking lot. We're accustomed to cleaning it, putting some Neosporin on it, bandaging it, and waiting a few days. Even that level of treatment here is like performing surgery.

By mid-morning, things shift. People from the village notice we're handing out things like Tylenol and Pedialyte. They stop being interested in getting treatment and start being concerned with scoring as much free shit as they can get their hands on. When we start to notice men getting back in line for another bottle of "head medicine" or "belly medicine," we tell them no. We have a limited amount of supplies and the bigger guys are using their size to gain a monopoly on them. This is something we see when we toss candy to the local kids from our Humvee while returning from missions. The biggest kids literally inflict physical violence on the smaller children to get a bottle of water or Tootsie Roll.

When the local men realize we caught on to them, they adapt. They begin sending in wave after wave of adorable, dirty little kids. One little girl with a gold flower piercing in her nose catches my eye. She's maybe five years old, but has the courageous soul of a warrior. She walks right up and tugs on a guy's pant leg and looks up with eyes that work like a microwave does to a stick of butter. None among us is a match for the little girl. She gets her hands on more band aids and topical antibiotics than aisle nine at Walgreens. Suckers, all of us.

By early afternoon we've run out of supplies and call for a resupply drop. A pallet of water bottles and MREs drop from the back of a C-130 and explode about a kilometer outside of the village. We dispatch a squad to recover the contents. We distribute what we can before making our way out of the village. Moving down the mountain with far less weight and a little daylight makes the exfil much more enjoyable than the movement up. Regardless of the benevolent nature of our visit, there's still a hypervigilance as we move toward the extraction point. I for one am not thrilled about being exposed on uneven terrain during the day. The uneasy feeling knowing we can take fire at any moment is enough to drown out the expansive beauty of our surroundings.

We're picked up without incident and make another long cold, cramped, nighttime helicopter ride that would be the highlight of any young boy's childhood; most of us just pass out on the frigid metallic floor of the rumbling bird. We land in Bagram with just enough time to make the last five minutes of midrats. A few of us take the opportunity to load up on individual boxes of cereal and paper containers of goat milk. The new season of *The O.C.* just dropped, so we're in for a long night. After our Chinook power nap and fresh stockpile of Froot Loops, we're up for the task.

Not much transpires over the following weeks. We do what Rangers do during slow deployment times. We go to the gym, play video games, get yelled at for tanning in our short silkies. Under the cover of darkness, I break into one of the B-huts where the SEALs live and steal several boxes of their complimentary Pop-Tarts. Despite being on the largest US military base in Afghanistan, we're completely segregated from the rest of the military. We don't pull gate guard shifts and for the most part don't abide by the rules of the rest of the Army. When we're in the states we never interacted with the rest of the military, but to some degree, we have to on this base.

We share a chow hall and a running track. It's common to have a First Sergeant or Sergeant Major from another unit stop us because we're in a different uniform, or our rifle has a bunch of gadgets on it they've never seen. I get yelled at during a sixteen-mile run for not having a reflective belt on by a guy who I assume has never actually been on a mission before.

I respond, "So the Taliban can't see me!" and continue my run.

Our next major mission of the deployment doesn't come for several more weeks. What started as an action-packed trip turns into another long, grinding tour, until one night when we all gather together before boarding the helicopters.

"Well, this isn't good," I hear from one of the squad leaders.

"What's going on?" I ask.

"The JSOC chaplain wants to pray for us before we leave on this mission."

"That's a first! It's probably because we're all going to die," jokes one of the senior privates.

"Sounds about right," chimes in another.

The sense of humor is as dark as one may expect from men who've been to combat several times before reaching the legal drinking age. I'm accustomed to it. I was exposed to similar grit as a kid in the fire stations of Peoria, Arizona. However, these are nineteen- and twenty-year-olds who are talking like the firefighters who are friends of my father. Those men witnessed twenty years of carnage to become that cynical. In just a couple of years of war-fighting they've already become as callous as men working civilian EMS for decades.

I image the speech delivered by the chaplain is a heartfelt one. I'm too busy trying to figure out how to work my radio to pay attention. Up until this point I've somehow managed to avoid having to carry a radio on mission. To be honest, I don't think I need one for this objective, either, but at this point I'm the only NCO in the platoon without one. As a medic I frequently get away with things that other NCOs don't, not intentionally of course. I finally get it to work as we board the Chinook helicopters for what will be my first hostage rescue mission.

Tucked between my body armor and plate carrier is a 3'x5' American flag. I want to give a gift to my father upon returning from this deployment that's significant, something to say "thank you for all you've done to support me." I figure carrying the flag of our country on a historically significant mission will suffice.

Parts of the following story are redacted for security reasons

We're informed that a _____ contractor has been captured by Taliban forces in the _____ province of Afghanistan. During the Operation Order I ask if the hostage has any medical conditions to consider. I'm told he has asthma, so I locate and add an albuterol inhaler to my packing list. I also add a couple of Red Bulls to my pack. The clock is ticking, but as important as speed is to the success of the mission, accuracy is just as crucial. With these types of missions, the stakes are a great deal higher than a direct action kill/capture objective. Our platoon's role is to be infilled a couple of clicks outside of the village to act as an immediate backup plan for the SEALs doing a high-altitude free-fall parachute (HALO) jump onto the objective.

The flight from BAF is the longest I've ever experienced in a helo. We're pulled off target multiple times so as to not compromise the SEAL's infill. We hover around in the back of the cramped Chinook literally all night. We took off at just after sunset and finally arrive on objective minutes before the sun comes up. My entire body cramps up in the heat of the Afghan night. There's guys on top of guys in the back of the stagnant floating bus. Nowhere to move for hours. Despite the uncomfortable conditions, no one complains. By the time we land my legs have completely seized up. I muster everything I have to simply run off the back gate into the desert night.

We form a semicircle around the back of our rotary winged aircraft to provide rear security for its take off. After hours of incessant noise and vibration it's completely silent, a shift so severe it sends a shiver up my spine. We sit in place holding security for at least twenty minutes; everyone is on high alert. The sun begins to illuminate the silhouettes of a few of the Rangers to my left and right. It's difficult to tell through the night vision goggles, but as soon as the day becomes brighter, it's evident we are, from a tactical standpoint, in about the worst possible place imaginable. We're sitting completely exposed on a hill with absolutely no cover or concealment. Ridges to three sides of us feature large rock formations ideal for enemy sniper positions. Missions like these do not require an officer above the rank of platoon leader; however, it is common for higher-ranking officers to add themselves to the manifest.

They do nothing but get in the way and more often than not, are present solely for the glory, for medals, and as a means by which to potentially achieve their next promotion. Not all officers are this way, but the majority I work with over the rank of captain fit the bill. The one who egotistically placed himself on this mission is all that and more. Because he's the highest-ranking guy on the ground, he assumes he should call the shots. He has less than half the combat experience of the youngest private in our platoon and it shows. His decision is to do nothing. We sit on an exposed piece of ground for hours in the burning sun with no cover. No information is disseminated to the members of the platoon. We sit for six hours waiting for orders and get burned beyond belief. Finally the decision is made to move into the rocks for cover.

By this point our platoon is dehydrated and pissed off. We receive an update that the Taliban has moved the hostage into the hills where we're located. We send out small patrol elements to search the area, but initially come up with nothing.

Eventually _____'s tragic fate is discovered. Someone in the village tipped off the hostage takers about American presence in the village. Three Taliban members then took their hostage into the hills just outside of the village and cut off his head was with an old band saw. We secure his body in the thick black bag intended for these occasions.

We call for exfil, but are denied. We're told that it is too dangerous. The 160th has already lost too many birds this rotation, and they won't touch down until they can do so under the cover of darkness. I know the logic behind the decision, but it still upsets me. We have over thirty guys exposed like sitting ducks. Our lives are trivialized in the grand scope of the fight. It's better to leave us out here than risk losing another helo. I understand the decision, but it doesn't make it any less shitty.

Now the hunger pains stab at me. My low blood sugar affects my ability to move. At this point we've been awake for well over thirty hours and still have at least another six on the rocks. *Oh shit, I forgot about those Red Bulls!* The can nearly burns my hand as I pull it from my pack. *Down the hatch!* I feel my blood sugar instantly rise and I become alert for the first time since we exited the Chinook. The high is short-lived, however. Within an hour of dusk, I crash. I crash hard! I can't focus at all; I'm going to pass out. I didn't pack any food because this was supposed to be a quick in-and-out. The mission plan called for us to be extracted by dawn. Stupid.

In the hundred missions I conduct after this one, I never make that same stupid mistake. Food becomes as essential on my packing list as ammo, regardless of how short the mission is supposed to be. I ask my buddy Nick if he has anything to eat. I feel terrible doing this because I'm supposed to be the one looking out for him and now I am asking for help. He produces a Harvest Bar from his assault pack and tosses it to me. He might as well have tossed me a Thanksgiving dinner with all the trimmings. It's strawberry and hard as a rock. Most strawberry foods are delicious, but strawberry Harvest Bars taste like absolute shit under most circumstances. Not this time though. I'm so grateful for the small piece of food. I don't think I would have maintained combat effectiveness without balancing out my blood sugar with that bar. Still to this day, I swear it saved my life.

What could have been another beautiful Afghan sunset is ignored as our platoon positions itself for exfil. I volunteer to help carry the man's remains to the bird. The flight crew takes the body bag containing _____. My platoon sergeant and I form a choke point at the tail of the helo to count everyone as they get on. Over the deafening churning of the rotor blades overhead I yell, "WE'RE UP SERGEANT!" I'm the last one to board and try to find a spot in the packed Chinook; there's no place to sit. Except. Except on the body bag. It's a sweltering four-hour flight back to Bagram Air Field. I spend the last few hours of that very long day sitting on top of our failed mission.

Our platoon conducts a few other missions over deployment, but we spend the majority of our time training. We have the opportunity to travel to another unit's compound in the mountains. It's a surreal experience having the opportunity to work with them. Their facility is incredible. Tucked into the mountain landscape, the work they conduct is amazing. They have their own mock villages set up for practicing raids, complete with fully furnished houses. We practice close quarter combat and live tissue training with their unit. I wish I could talk about it in further detail; however, in an effort to respect the secret nature of what they do I must refrain.

We frequently find ourselves at a spot known as East River Range. It isn't much of a shooting range to speak of. It's more like a place out in the desert. Just a dirt road leading to a lot of open desert with a mountain backdrop. There's never a shortage of ammo to shoot. Being the medic, I'm able to float around and cross train with all the different weapon systems. The guys from our mortar section are eager to teach me how to lob a 60mm a few hundred meters. The snipers teach with the proficiency of a college professor on windage and trajectory and all their various tools. I throw several rounds through the Barrett 50 caliber, which, needless to say, is cool as fuck! The breachers show me all the ways they use to gain access to a building including the shotgun, Halligan and C-4 charge. We shoot anti-tank rockets and deploy Claymore mines and throw grenades.

As cool as all that is, none of it is as fun as shooting the MK19 grenade launcher. The MK19 is a belt-fed, air-cooled, fully automatic truck-mounted grenade launcher capable of hucking up to sixty grenades per minute at a distance of up to two kilometers. Typically you fire that piece of war glory in six to nine round bursts, then you wait. The rounds float in the air like a fadeaway jump shot. Since light travels faster than sound, the operator gets to see the impact of the half dozen grenades a couple of seconds before hearing their explosion. I can still feel my belly jiggle from laughing like a young child at the joy exuded from firing that weapon.

We continue to grow as a platoon, teaching one another the skills we've become specialists in. As I teach the men in my platoon first responder skills, they teach me how to do their jobs. We gain a more comprehensive proficiency as a unit. We will need every bit of that proficiency if we're going to survive our next deployment.

Shortly after my twenty-third birthday (which I successfully keep a secret), I board the massive cargo plane to return home from Afghanistan for a second time.

Training force on force with sim rounds on Bagram Airfield.

Shooting mortars on East River Range

Ranger snipers Steve and Chris reaching out and touching some targets.

East River Range. My superiors always got pissed
when I referred to the AT4 as a bazooka.

CHAPTER 10

When Skeletons Live

"With friends like these, huh, Gary?"
The Dude

Within hours of stepping off the plane from Afghanistan I'm on my back porch with a beer in hand. It's early October. It doesn't feel like a minute has passed since Matt and I were planning our 4th of July BBQ, yet everything has changed. We catch up well into the morning hours. There's a unique weight to war. It piles on your back differently than the rest of life's collective events. There's no place for weakness while deployed, no time for reflection, and no room for sadness. Keep sharp, head on a swivel, always in the game. I'm home now and after a few drinks, the weight of compounding near death experiences has its way with me.

Matt sits with me on the ground in our backyard as I unload, brick by brick, everything I've carried from our first mission to our last day in country. My hands tremble and I'm on the verge of tears when he provides me a great deal of solace with one simple statement. "You know man, that's just the way it is. Things will never be the same."

I'm not sure why, but it's comforting, almost familiar. It makes me feel like I'm not alone in my pain. Matt's always been a good friend, but never much of a philosopher, so his words catch me by surprise. Before going to bed, Matt asks me if I want to go to a Notre Dame game the following weekend.

"We can fly into Chicago and catch a ride to South Bend with a friend of mine. My parents have season tickets. You have a four-day weekend next week, right?"

"Yeah. That sounds perfect, bud. Let's make that happen." I stay up and finish the case of beer. When Matt wakes up he realizes I haven't gone to sleep at all. My mind is a tornado, spinning dissonant with the loom of war.

"You wanna get breakfast?" he asks

"Sure," I slur. It's the first meal in months I won't have to carry a weapon to. As we get into Matt's Jeep, his iPod kicks on, *"I'd love to go back to when we played as kids, but things change and that's just the way it is. That's just the way it is, things will never be the same, that's just the way it is awww yeah."*

"Are you fucking kidding me, Matt?"

"What?"

"Last night when I was trying to process all that shit you quoted me Tupac? What the fuck, man?!" Matt just shrugs his shoulders and backs out of the driveway. That's the thing about Matt Voll; if anyone else pulls the shit he does, you'd hate them for it, but he somehow always manages to come off like such a comedian you can't help but laugh.

Driving to IHOP, I notice how smooth the roads are in this country. No massive holes to avoid from IEDs, the lanes are clearly marked, and people pay attention to the traffic signals. It makes me feel out of place and highly uncomfortable. The sense of heightened vigilance becomes like a blanket. When the cold harsh winter months turn to summer, the habit of that blanket becomes uncomfortable, yet for some reason you continue to cloak yourself in it. You don't want to look over your shoulder constantly; it's just become such a necessary habit, it stays with you. You live in it. Sweltering.

The next few days at work are standard for having just returned from rotation. We lay out equipment and count everything. Certain items have to be cleaned and returned. The days are short by Ranger standards. We have a late work call each day, which means we don't have to be in until six, and we're released by one in the afternoon. It's common to have a couple of four-day weekends before block leave. Block leave is a required two-week vacation the entire Battalion takes simultaneously. For the sake of unit readiness, we don't get to choose when we take vacation.

I can't wait for this weekend. I've never been to a college football game, but I know Notre Dame will be one hell of a good time. Matt grew up in South Bend, Indiana. He's the oldest of five Irish brothers. When we arrive at his parent's house they welcome me like a sixth son. Matt's family is amazing. I met Matt's father at his Ranger school graduation the previous spring. His mother emerges from the kitchen as we enter the house. "Hello, you must be Jenkins."

The thought of my friend's mother calling me by my last name doesn't seem odd to me at this point. She gives me a big hug then steps back and looks at me. "I thought you would be bigger."

I'm not sure how to take that exactly. They've prepared a huge BBQ for Matt's homecoming. Matt's friends from college roll in one by one to welcome him home. I feel like I already know so many of them from the stories Matt tells. Apparently, Matt must've told them stories about me as well, because more than one of them upon meeting me comments, "You're Jenkins? Holy shit! I thought you'd be bigger."

We make a serious dent in the beer stash Matt's parents keep in their garage before heading out to the bar. As we walk into the pub, Matt asks if I've ever seen *Rudy*. Without waiting for me to respond, he explains several of the scenes in the movie were shot in this bar. I could give shit, I just want a drink. Matt's parents come out to the bar with us. I'm not sure if it's because they miss him and want to spend time with him or if it's because they know he will do something stupid, and despite his position as an Army Ranger, they still feel the need to look after him.

The bar is crowded. It's the first time I feel anxious in this environment. I choose a table toward the corner so my back can face the wall. I take responsibility for the first round and bring a heavy tray to our table, loaded down with eight Irish Car Bombs. It's a good start on the evening as we clink glasses and shout an old toast. *Here's to the breezes . . .* We have a great time reminiscing. I get to hear all kinds of new stories about Matt. Apparently he was banned from this very bar years before for attempting to kidnap a midget. As the story goes, he scooped the little guy up in his overcoat and ran out the door with him. The stories his parents tell fit perfectly with the person who I've been living with.

Things are going well for the first hour. Up to this point in the evening Matt behaves himself, which is why it's so odd when he walks back to our table and calmly says, "Well, I'm getting kicked out of here in 5, 4, 3, 2 . . ."

Before he gets to one, the bouncer grabs him by the shoulder. "Alright smart guy, you're out of here!"

What the fuck? I think to myself. No one at the table has any clue what's going on or why Matt's being told to leave. I quickly follow them to the front door asking what my friend did to get tossed out. The bouncer was clearly a Marine. I can tell by his tattoos and stupid haircut. I ask him again. This time he responds by yelling, "You want me to throw you out, too?"

"No, asshole, I want to know why you are throwing my friend out. I'd also like to know why you think you can talk to me that way?" That gets his attention! By this time we're right outside the front door and I'm surrounded by four security guys. Two of them are overweight and clearly got the job because they're large, the third guy is a buck fifty soaking wet. The only one I'm mildly concerned with is the tattooed Marine. Our indignant exchange goes on for a couple of minutes before Matt's parents come out to see what's happening.

"Where is Matt?" asks his mother.

Wait a minute, where is Matt? Did he really just get me mixed up in all of this and wander off?!

Matt's mother urges me to walk away but I'm in full-blown tough guy mode and won't be reasoned with. I respond, "It's alright, Mrs. Voll, there's only four of them. Easy day!"

In all reality I'm about to get my ass kicked, but my bluff works because they back up and head inside. Matt comes walking up with a sack full of Taco Bell and a gordita hanging out of his mouth.

"Are you fucking kidding me, Matt!? I'm about to fight four guys for God knows what and you went to get a fucking gordita!"

He just shrugs his shoulders as he turns and walks to his parent's blue minivan. On the way back to his house, we ask Matt what that was all about. Apparently the bartender is a college nemesis of Matt's, so under the portion on his tab labeled 'tip' he scribbled in "blow me, asshole." A collective sigh and head shake is shared between his parents and me. None of us are remotely surprised by his actions.

Matt and I pass out on the couches in his parent's basement. The next morning I'm startled awake by something touching my nose. I grab at it with my left hand and swing with my right! My eyes open mid swing to see it's Matt's mother playing a joke. I manage to stop the swing just in time. I'm still incredibly jumpy from my last deployment. The thought of those A-10s dropping payload on the Taliban fighters during Operation Red Wings floods my mind and I'm instantly transported back, still clenching her wrist.

As Matt sits up I hear him say, "I told you not to fuck with him while he's sleeping." It takes a few moments for my heart rate to return to under a hundred beats per minute. "Breakfast is ready," she says as she walks up the stairs, startled from nearly getting punched in the face.

It's early, but not too early to start our tailgating. A quick breakfast of sausage and beer and we're on our way to see some college football at Notre Dame! It's surprisingly close, maybe a five-minute drive from their home. One of Matt's younger brothers is already there setting up a giant inflatable penguin atop his red Dodge Ram. He filled the back with sand for a festive beach theme. There's hundreds, if not thousands, of cars and trucks set up for the tailgate festivities. I've never seen anything like it. College sports are not as important where I grew up.

People have the most extravagant setups just to get drunk before a sporting event. There's no way we will find Patrick in this chaos. Then we see it, standing out among the green and gold leprechauns, the ten-foot-tall inflatable Christmas penguin. Okay, now it makes sense. In all, there's about a dozen of us, mostly Matt's college buddies. It doesn't take long before the large bottles of whiskey start getting passed around. I take a massive pull out of one while standing in the back of Patrick's truck. Mid-swig I see four police officers on horseback stroll up. "HOLY SHIT! It's the Four Horsemen of the

Apocalypse! This is it, the end of days!" I yell, in a slurred tone. They signal for me to sit down, unamused. I oblige willingly.

We're in the parking lot for five hot dogs, eight beers, and several pulls of whiskey. By now, many of the people from our group have already entered the stadium. The game is set to begin and the horse-mounted cops are trying to get people inside. As we enter the stadium the sheer magnitude of the place engulfs me. Matt informs me we will be sitting in the donor section. I'm not entirely sure what he means. We walk up a dark corridor to where our seats are.

The experience of seeing the field and tens of thousands of screaming fans is an assault on my senses. It stops me in my tracks. I've never seen anything like this in my life. Matt just slurs, "Pretty fucking cool ain't it?" The usher takes us to our seats. We keep descending, step after step, row after row. We're getting closer and closer to the field. We get to the gate directly behind the players on the thirty-five-yard line. We have the first two rows! I look back and see a sea of green and gold. It feels like there's a thousand rows of excited Irish fans behind us. Apparently the donor section is reserved for people who donate a significant amount of money to the university. There's a couple of famous people sitting in the rows behind ours, one of whom is a very popular morning talk show TV personality.

I can't believe where I am right now. Just last week I was sleeping on a cot in a third-world country. Again, I feel out of place. The sheer number of people makes me feel uncomfortable. A first quarter Notre Dame touchdown helps put me at ease. Right before the extra point is kicked I'm told the tradition is to hoist someone up onto the group's shoulders and have them do an equal number of push-ups as points on the board. I'm nominated and willingly accept. This irritates the people behind us who paid a lot for their seats. It irritates them even more when we score again within a few minutes and I'm back up on my friend's shoulders, this time without a shirt on. "Sit down!" the hordes holler at us.

Patrick, a student at Notre Dame, responds with volatility, "FUCK YOU, STAND UP!" Well, that doesn't go over so well.

We're given our first warning, a warning we immediately brush off. Every time a good play is made we stand and cheer, an action which pisses off the over-privileged, entitled "fans" sitting behind us.

We're playing BYU, so needless to say, I'm getting a lot of push-ups in. By the third or fourth time security has to come back to our seats they tell Patrick he has to leave with them. Once again I interject and ask why, and once again I get pulled into the fray. We're both removed from our seats and escorted to the area where they sell overpriced hot dogs. The volunteer security guy starts to give Patrick and me a speech about integrity and responsibility. I stand, arms crossed, head tilted to the side, essentially displaying a big *fuck you* with my body language. After he says some line about how we should learn to grow up I think about everything I've been through in the last three months and I let out a laugh. The guy turns his attention from Patrick and looks me up and down. He inquires, "Is there something about this that is funny to you, son?"

"Sir," I reply, "I'm sure there are plenty of things in this world I find funny that you don't. This is certainly one of them." Well, that pisses him off just the right amount. Fortuitously enough, a police officer is walking by at just this moment. The volunteer hall monitor in the borrowed yellow security shirt informs the officer that we are heavily intoxicated and need to go. I just nod my head as I'm being flexed cuffed by officer friendly. Hmm, so this is what zip ties feel like. I've snapped flex cuffs on a few terrorist assholes in the past; having them cinched around my wrists feels pretty ironic.

As the officer escorts us to the in-stadium holding cell, which is about a three minute walk, we get hooted at by several of the game's patrons. Patrick holds his bound hands in the air and yells, "I guess we love the Irish just a little too much! I guess we cheered just a little too loud!" The people we pass go crazy and cheer for us. I just shake my head and think, *please Patrick, shut up.*

When we arrive at the holding cell the officer asks us what happened. Patrick explains with amazing inaccuracy about half of what actually took place. At some point he tells the officer I just returned from Afghanistan a couple of days prior, a fact the officer takes interest in. He asks my unit and my rank, my job, and my time in service. I'm candid and forthright with my answers, a tactic I believe he appreciates. He tells us he was in the 101st Airborne Division while administering a breathalyzer test. Now, I haven't failed a test probably since grade school, but this one is sure to mess with my GPA. We started drinking at seven this morning and it's almost three in the afternoon. "Point zero seven," the officer says.

How the fuck is that possible? Even the officer is shocked. This goes against what the hall monitor told him about us being completely wasted. He begins to believe Patrick's story a little more. Paired with the camaraderie of being paratroopers, he decides to let us go.

"So we can go back to our seats then?"

"Ha! Not a chance," he replies. "You can go home."

"Just so we're clear here officer, right now what you're telling me is I'm not too drunk to drive home, but I am too drunk to go back to the college football game?"

"Yep, but I don't suggest you drive right now."

As Patrick and I have our cuffs removed, we are released directly into the parking lot. The first thing we see is a bar called Legends. It's in the same parking lot as the stadium.

"Well, Patrick, he said not to drive right now. We should probably go in there and sit down for a little while, what do you think?"

"Maybe get a cocktail or two?"

"You read my mind, buddy."

Two weeks later we both receive certified letters from the University of Notre Dame stating:

> *"Dear Mr. Jenkins,*
> *Based upon a report by Notre Dame Security Police, I have determined that your presence on the grounds of the University of Notre Dame can no longer be permitted."*

It went on with some other legal jargon. That letter hangs framed above my toilet to this day. Patrick is the second Voll brother to get me banned for life from a respected establishment.

The next six months of training are considerably more exciting than my first cycle. There's a lot of the same stuff as before, but additionally I get into a few advanced schools. One of which being a tactile fighting school called Vanguard. About a dozen of us show up in Chicago to spend two full weeks learning hand to hand striking, knife fighting and advanced tactical firearms training. It's two of the most valuable weeks of non-medical training I receive as a Ranger. We're put through several scenarios each day mimicking situations we're likely to find ourselves in. We walk from one side of a large room to the other, through a crowd of a couple of dozen individuals. Two of whom are given the direction to attack unprovoked. There's no way of knowing who the attacker will be.

"Embrace the violence!" is all the instructor shouts as two men pounce from behind. I started the course with a broken nose and a large gash over my eye from an MMA bout I competed in the night prior to departing for Chicago. I won the fight, but you can't tell by looking at me. The super glue holding my eyebrow together consistently breaks apart throughout the course, sending a steady stream of blood into my eyes.

At night we explore the streets of Chicago, battered and bruised from the day's training. Early each morning we return to the gym for further advanced combatives training. The course concludes with an opportunity to go head to head in a shoot house with another government agency with MP5s retrofitted as paintball guns and dowling rods for knives. I learn as much about close quarter combat in one day as over two deployments.

I also have the distinct privilege of attending my second hospital rotation, this time in Atlanta at Grady. There's only two of us this time and we're only the second group to come through. As a result, most of the hospital staff has no clue how to treat us. Most of them treat us like paramedics and never inquire to our level of training. Being a special operations medic is a double-edged sword. Through the course of your training and experience you become one of the most capable, well-rounded medical personnel in the world, yet no one outside of your tiny community has a clue as to what you are capable of. As a result you are treated like an EMT Basic and told to hold the patient's head when they come in with multi-systems trauma.

There are exceptions to this, however. Our preceptor for this rotation is a brilliant surgeon named Doctor Jeff Salomone. He gives us reign to do whatever procedures we feel comfortable doing. I have the opportunity to treat more gunshot wounds during the three weeks than the collective previous three years. The two weeks of fourteen-hour days at Grady Hospital prove to be priceless for what's about to come.

By early 2006, I'd promoted to Sergeant, and my platoon earned the top spot as the primary battalion effort after a top performance at platoon evaluations. Platoon evals is a three-day training event testing every aspect of a platoon's combat effectiveness and capability. With the exception of a couple of brand new privates who just joined our platoon, our entire element has several combat deployments. We've refined our ability to communicate with one another, making our element a well-oiled machine. We'll need every bit of that proficiency as we step off the back of that cargo plane for the third time. This time into Tikrit, Iraq, at a period approaching the most violent in the history of the war.

Vanguard.

Violence of action

CHAPTER 11

Crossing the Frame

"War is old men talking, and young men dying."
~Franklin D. Roosevelt

It's hot. A different kind of hot than Georgia. That opening-the-preheated-oven-blast hot. The heat from the engine above us beats down on my shoulders as the heat from the desert floor below smashes back. We're caught in the crossfire, feet dangling in the breeze a hundred feet off the arid Iraq landscape. The heat is most of what I recall from each of my nighttime Black Hawk rides. Other than the heat, I suppose my mind is just swimming in adrenaline.

I look around at the other nine Rangers aboard. I'm trying to find something in their eyes, some emotion, some fear or anger. Fuckers are like seasoned poker players though. I hope my bluff is holding up. I hope they can't see my anxiety through the shadows.

"TWO MINUTES OUT!" someone screams and we echo back. I can't see the target house yet. Like a CD, my mind skips, and I'm kneeling behind a two-foot wall being drilled by pebbles as the Black Hawk takes off behind us. I'm here with my friend Nathan Ellis; he's the company comms chief now. He took over for Sgt. Patterson when he got out a while back. The assaulters are through the door so fast.

BOOM, POP, POP, POP.

The only time, and just for a brief second, a treacherous thought leaps into my cognition. *What if I can't save them?* The notion paralyzes me momentarily. I'm frozen in a terrifying moment of doubt. A technicolor symphony of flash bangs plays out twenty feet away. We receive the instructions to enter the building.

Another skip of the CD and I'm inside. The sound of children screaming is rattling. It's hotter inside the smoke-filled house than it was outside. There's a door directly to my left. It's where the screams are coming from. Like I'm walking on the bottom of the ocean, my steps are slow as I enter the room. A dozen children ranging from three to eleven cry out violently. Everyone who looks big enough to shoulder a weapon have been separated. Many of them are clenching their face and rolling on the ground. The heavy fog of gunpowder clogs my inhalation.

It takes a moment, but quickly I realize one of the guys tossed a nine-banger in the room, which is little more than nine blasts of loud noise and light used to stun the enemy. One by one, I check the children's faces. They are all completely fine, just scared shitless. We search the house quickly before the Blackhawks return. We take four detainees without a single injury on either side. Yet another skip of the CD and we are back on post in the After Action Review (AAR). I have nothing to add to the brief, but my heart's still pounding. I feel like we were just in this room five minutes ago receiving the pre-mission brief. It all went so fast. JOC, helicopter, wall, kids, detainees, helicopter, JOC.

If things keep up like this, Iraq is going to be a pretty easy deployment.

CHAPTER 12

Gravemakers and Gunslingers

"Gentlemen, prepare to defend yourselves."

"Hey, Doc, wake up!"

"I wasn't . . ." I can't even finish saying I wasn't sleeping. The door slams shut and Josh moves on to wake up the next CHU (Combat Housing Unit, pronounced *chew*), an eight foot by eight foot, jail cell-like, Conex box we live in while working in the torrid summer heat of Tikrit, Iraq. NCOs and officers get their own rooms, privates typically have to double up. Even with two overgrown Ranger privates in the eight-by-eight, these are still, hands down, the best living conditions I've experienced on any of my deployments.

This must be important; Josh usually talks shit for at least a couple of minutes. I glance over at the clock. It's 1600 so most of our guys are just waking up. I poke my head out of the door to see a handful of guys headed to the makeshift plywood Joint Operations Center (JOC).

"What's up?"

"Come on, Doc, let's go. Mission brief in five."

As usual I have no clue what's going on. Even now as a Sergeant, I somehow still seem to evade the chain of information passing through the platoon. I decide shower shoes aren't the best footwear choice for this occasion and quickly get dressed. I walk into the JOC just in time to not get more than a dirty look from my platoon sergeant. I half-heartedly listen while a certain officer who most everyone in our company maintains a great disdain for babbles on about two guys in a safehouse who are our primary kill/capture objectives. We'll fast rope in utilizing UH60 Black Hawk helicopters. He says some other things, but I'm focused on my empty stomach. Waking up to a kill/capture mission brief at this point in the deployment is as routine as bacon and eggs. We've only been in Iraq for a month and have already executed dozens of successful direct action missions. The pattern doesn't change. Why should it? It works. As a result, the missions blur together.

Wheels up at 1900. By the time the major finishes his bloviating, we have a little under two hours to eat and get our mission essentials together. For me that means making sure I have plenty of snacks in my "morale pouch." A watermelon Jolly Rancher given at the proper time is better than Christmas morning to a six-year-old when you've been on an objective for two days. Half of being a good medic is about keeping up the morale of your guys.

The boys from the 160th Special Operations Aviation Regiment (SOAR) pick us up right on time, which as usual is just past sundown. They're as nocturnal as soldiers come, and more than once I've been grateful for their outstanding ability to operate under the dark of night. The feeling of letting your feet dangle out of the door of a Black Hawk helicopter a couple of hundred feet off the deck is unmatched. However, today I'm pushed to the back jump seat, which means I'll be one of the last guys on the ground.

The flight is short and the hot night air feels good as it swirls around the inside of the bird. The heat from the engine reminds me of standing next to the oven while my grandmother made cookies. Tattered combat boots punch the arid desert sand, two at a time, until the Black Hawk is empty. Josh quickly positions his fire team to move toward the front door. The bird pulls away, showering us all with BB-sized pebbles and debris from the open field. Eyes, nose, and mouth are caked with ancient soil, obstructing the senses momentarily.

We're less than one hundred meters to the target house as we begin to advance. Second squad approaches from the side of the building. Weapons squad is set in a blocking position behind the target house in the event anyone attempts to run. As I move closer to the tiny, desolate house in the middle of the field, it happens . . .

I feel the heat from the blast from forty meters away. Everything is a white, high-pitched buzzing and then, silence. There's nothing. Time stops. I wait to hear someone scream out, medic. I wait for something. Anything. Every ounce of air escapes my now-vacant lungs. I wait, a lifetime in that single breath, I wait. As my eyes regain focus I realize the blast came from the exact position where second squad was just in. The predator drone feed in the JOC shows the heat pattern from the blast completely white out the screen and erase the six Rangers who stood within a couple of meters of the suicide bomber's position.

Air rapidly enters my lungs the way it does after you've been held under water a little too long. I look immediately to my platoon sergeant and we run. Not to cover, not to safety, but directly at that shack of a house in the middle of that field, in the middle of nowhere. Josh's fire team reaches the front door just in time to receive a volley of 7.62 slung at them from a RPK set up on the other side of the shack's mud wall.

They don't hesitate. They act. They run into the throat of the monster, directly through the door with the business end of a very large automatic weapon pointed at it. At the helm of that weapon is a man hell bent on their demise. They don't hesitate. They act. At this moment I notice someone running from the objective directly toward weapons squad's position. The only thought in my mind is second squad disappearing at the hand of a suicide bomber.

I raise my rifle. It's dark and he's seventy-five meters away. The green beam illuminating from my PEC-2, only visible by night vision goggles, finds his chest. *Go on and pull that trigger. Squeeze. Squeeze.* I instinctively come to a complete stop to take the two shots. Rifles are cackling in all directions. As the figure drops I continue to run. I'm not entirely sure why, but I change directions. Instead of running toward the front door, I begin to run to the motionless body that just a breath ago was standing. I'm within fifteen meters. *BOOM!*

I feel a second blast. This one's much closer. My exposed face is peppered by what feels like tiny ball bearings. I stay on my feet; my eyes never lose focus of the white tunic laying forty-five feet in front of me. It's a blast from a frag grenade thrown by my good friend Allen in an effort to clear the back room of the shack. The sound of controlled pairs popping off hasn't stopped by the time I reach him. They rattle like a combat symphony. For the second time in the longest minute of my life, my breath is stolen from me. He's a boy, he's just a boy, and he's still breathing. He has six holes in him. He's been shot from multiple positions.

I don't remember the next few minutes. The world keeps moving and I'm assuming I do, too, because the next thing I know I'm kneeling over one of the members of second squad talking with another medic named John Graves. It's his first deployment, but he's as squared-away as they come.

He's okay. A suicide vest detonated within spitting distance and he's okay; how the hell is he alive? As I look up I see Thomas, second squad leader. He's directing the rest of his guys. They're alive. They're all alive! How? I'm at a total loss for words in this moment. I'm not a pious man, but in this moment I'd bet a fistful of Chipotle buy-one-get-ones those men were recipients of a little divine intervention.

I begin to tend to some of their minor wounds when I remember first squad taking heavy fire upon entering the building. I hand over care to John and quickly make my way to the front door. The mangled flatbed truck where the suicide bomber sat up and proclaimed "allahu akbar" is forever seared into my mind. I see what appears to be his legs and most of his body. His head is completely gone. My best guess is the vest was poorly constructed and the brunt of the blast traveled up rather than out. His head is found, intact, thirty meters away; popped off like the cork of a cheap bottle of Champagne. I reach the front door. The small room is quickly cleared by the guys from first squad, who are now in search mode. I ask if everyone is okay. All I get is a couple of uneasy laughs. Apparently one of the 7.62 rounds grazed one of the younger guy's helmets.

The room is small and filled with smoke from the gunfight. There's a hole just big enough for a man to crawl through in the back corner of the room.

Apparently several men crawled through the hole to another room as first squad made entry into the first room. After eliminating the threat on the RPK, Allen tossed a frag grenade into the back room rather than chase the men on his hands and knees. I joke with him that nearly blowing me up in the process will cost him a beer when we get stateside. He just shrugs his shoulders as if to say, *welcome to the 'I just got blown up club.'*

There's a couple of mangled, lifeless bodies on the floor in the front room. One is slumped over the machine gun; the other must have drawn the short straw. He got to be the last guy to crawl through the room's only egress. Just as my desire to poke them with a stick draws me one step into the room, I hear my call signal on the radio. It's my platoon sergeant. Second squad is chasing someone that our eye in the sky spots fleeing the target house. I immediately run to their location. By the time I get there, the company commander is giving an order to my good friend Nick Pence.

Nick and I both promoted to sergeant at the same time. Nick is an exceptional Ranger. In addition to saving my life with that disgusting strawberry Harvest Bar in Afghanistan, he's smart, well-spoken, and liked among the guys. Several factors contributing to his quick promotion. He's also very good at taking orders . . . normally.

Second squad discovered one of the men pinned down in a reservoir. The company commander wants Nick to send one of the guys on his team down into the reservoir to grab the guy and try to pull him up the steep muddy side that's about eight feet high.

In the kind of tone you expect a Ranger Sergeant to address a superior officer, Nick asks, "Sir, you want me to send one of my guys who just got blown up by a suicide bomber into that hole and grab another potential suicide bomber, throw him on his shoulder, and carry him up that eight foot mud wall?"

"Roger, Sergeant Pence."

That's what the CO wants, but that's not what happens. Nick responds the way a respected Ranger should. I'll never forget what occurs next, and I will not repeat here.

Just about the time the incident is resolved, another call comes over the radio requesting my presence on the north side of the target house. As I approach, I see Eric, Nathan, and our interpreter standing over the shot boy. He's still breathing, in fact he's talking. As I kneel down to assess his wounds I ask the interpreter what he's saying. I notice he has more than just two holes in him. He was hit from multiple shooters. For some reason I now feel less responsible for his situation. The interpreter tells us the kid is fourteen and came to Iraq from Saudi Arabia. I ask him what he's doing in Iraq. As long as I live I will never forget our exchange, the dry Iraq dirt caking my mouth, the fresh blood escaping his.

"I have come here to kill Americans!"

"Then why did you run?"

"There are too many."

"How did you get here?"

"They paid me to come."

"What would your parents think if they knew that you were here?"

"They would be proud."

Without hesitation, I turn and walk away. I have the power to help and do nothing. To this day I have yet to fully process this decision. Guilt? Shame? Ambivalence? I don't know how to feel about it. I'm not sure what emotion to affix to such an event. I know he lived because of the efforts of another medic, but I did nothing—an inaction which still keeps me up some nights.

As I walk back to the target house, I see the severed head of the suicide bomber, fully intact. It doesn't even phase me, I just walk by it. Once back in the house I link up with my friends from first squad. They've just finished searching the house for any possible links to other cells in the area. The place is an absolute mess. I notice something that I can't help but laugh about. At the feet of one of the dead terrorist lay a couple of bottles of a *7UP* knock-off drink called *CHEER UP*. I pick it up and first squad's team leader, Matt Sanders, takes a quick picture. He cracks a joke, "Feeling down about getting blown the fuck up? Have a refreshing glass of *CHEER UP!*"

Josh Lashley, the other team leader in first squad, takes a bottle back home to the States and uses its contents to make mixed drinks in his barrack room. Just as we call for exfil, a message comes over the radio. We're getting an add-on mission. Abu Musab al-Zarqawi was spotted less than one hundred miles away. At the time, Zarqawi is the Iraqi equivalent of Osama Bin Laden; he's high value target number one. We make our way back to the exfil point and wait for the Black Hawks to return. As we wait, a thermobaric bomb is dropped on the house, which served as a crucible for 1st platoon. The mud hut is erased from existence, but never from my memory.

No one speaks a word on the short helicopter ride to Balad. Call it exhaustion, or quiet reflection, just distant stares out into the lifeless night. Each member of the platoon steps off the bird and onto the tarmac at least two inches taller than when they woke up this morning. We walk through the doors of the hangar in the middle of the night as if we're one single organism.

There's a contingent of Rangers who just watched our entire mission from the drone feed. We're caked in dirt and blood and possess a newfound saltiness. As the adrenaline slowly wears off, I look to my left and right and see a certain grit in even the newest private in our platoon's eyes. One of those men is a Ranger named Nicholas Irving. I believe this is his first gunfight as a Ranger. It won't be his last. Irving eventually goes on to be one of the most well-known snipers in Special Operations. This being my final deployment as a Ranger, the moment feels like a passing of the torch. The things these young Rangers will learn on their first deployment will serve them well in the years to come.

There's a dozen old green cots set up in the hangar where men sit as they reload the black thirty-round magazines recently emptied. We replace the batteries in our night vision devices and top off our CamelBaks. I'm exhausted, but know the night is just getting started. The adrenaline is dumping and my legs feel heavier than normal. I'm amazed as I check over the members of second squad who just experienced what a suicide bomber tastes like. A few minor burns and scratches, but nothing beyond that.

As I finish treating some of the men with simple dressings, my platoon sergeant calls me into a small room in the back of the hangar. He hands me a box filled with atropine auto injector. (The AtroPen® Auto-Injector is indicated for the treatment of poisoning by nerve agents.) He asks me if I can give the platoon a short refresher on the use of the AtroPen and tells me

Zarqawi is believed to be held up in a chemical warehouse and is likely to use chemical weapons on our platoon as we enter.

It probably comes off as a pretty smartass comment, but I have to ask, "Sergeant, you want me to go out there and tell that group of guys there's a chance that, after all they've just been through, they may need to stab atropine into their own leg to keep from having their insides melt?"

He understands I'm being sincere. He knows I don't want to see those men put in harm's way again, but we both know that's our job. He doesn't say a word, he doesn't have to. I walk out from the back room and start handing out the little handheld injectors as though they're pieces of Halloween candy. I get a few confused looks, a lot of shoulder drops and headshakes, and one big fat grin. He knows I'm not handing these fuckers out as a joke, and I think he truly reveled in the idea of getting his hands a little dirtier.

The men stand with professionalism as I give a quick tutorial on how to self-administer the drug into the outside part of the thigh. At the end of the instruction, I ask if anyone has any questions; only one man speaks up.

"So, Doc, our faces might get melted off tonight?"

"It's a possibility," I respond.

"Cool."

Once again we climb aboard the Black Hawk helicopters en route to uncertainty. As we take flight we're informed the mission is being called off. Some of the men are disappointed, the ones with families are relieved, and the rest are indifferent. We all know the acts Zarqawi has committed warrant his absolute demise and every man aboard would love the opportunity to be the hand of vengeance. None in the group would hesitate to do so, but at the same time none of these men carry a death wish. Be smart in the way you hunt and you will live to hunt another day, become overzealous and you get replaced by a folded flag handed to your next of kin. Ironically enough, this would not be the platoon's last shot at Zarqawi, but for now it's time to call it a night.

CHAPTER 13

There Will be Justice in Murder

"Onward we stagger, and if the tanks come, may God help the tanks."
~Col. William Darby

Each twenty-four-hour period begins to look exactly like the one before. Wake up at three in the afternoon, go to the gym, check on any missions that could be developing, eat "dinner," and wait.

By sundown we check the batteries in our radios and ensure we have all the necessary supplies to get through another night raid. An hour or so after the sun sets we get picked up by a group of Black Hawks and are delivered to the doorstep of another jihadist.

One hundred nights of summer. A thousand chances to kill and just as many to die. One evening seems to stand out from the rest. We get intel on an individual who our big brothers have been tracking for a while. He's a tier-one target and has evaded capture for some time. The appropriate plans are made and once again we find ourselves with feet dangling from the open door, the hot summer desert air stinging our faces.

A split second before the bird touches down I hop from my position in the door of the Black Hawk. My feet welcome the embrace of the uneven soft dirt field. I know Allen and Josh will be racing me for this one. Getting to be the guy to pull the trigger on this particular shithead will be huge bragging rights. The people inside already know we're here. There's no way for them not to. Four UH60s just landed in their front yard. Tonight, speed is security. The faster we can get to the front door, the less time our enemy will have to prepare for the inevitable assault. Not that there's much you can do to prepare when thirty Rangers are running at your front door in the middle of the night. I get to the door a split second ahead of Allen, Josh, and SFC Straight. Somehow I end up as the third man in the stack.

We don't sit on the door, we flow instantly. We've rehearsed this hundreds if not thousands of times. Allen breaks left and controls the first corner; Josh enters the room and heads right. I follow Allen to the left and SFC Straight follows Josh to the right. Allen and I have a door directly in front of us. Without so much as a blink of hesitation we enter the interior door. A figure in the far corner is holding an AK47 oriented on the door we just entered with every intention of spraying us with 7.62mm rounds. As if it occurs in slow motion, his rifle jams, giving Allen the opportunity to acquire his target. The man fluidly transitions from his AK47 to a frag grenade. As his finger embraces the pin, he receives two perfectly placed rounds to the face, carrying the contents of his skull out the back of his head. He drops atop the grenade and we brace for impact. It doesn't explode.

Two more shots ring out from outside the room. Someone just engaged a target running toward the room we're in. Flash bangs pop as Rangers flow seamlessly through the house. This is the pinnacle of controlled chaos. Shots ring out from outside the target house. I can't help but think, *this must be what war feels like.* Every nerve fires in a perfect state of flow.

The pilots are precise and efficient with the infill of our two-team sniper element. Before the dust settles and the beat of the helo's rotors are gone, Alex, Myles, Isaiah, and Jake hear our shots cracking from inside. The fight commenced before they get into place. Alex sees a shadowy figure clumsily leap out of a window on the red side of the target and begins trotting in his direction. Ten green lasers converge on him. He has no idea he's running directly at a blocking position while holding an AK. He's running from the fight, leaving the men in the house to fall at our hands. He's met with a wall of lead, his bodily functions turn off like a light switch. A terrified look of fear permanently frozen on the face of Hamadi Tahki, the high value target we're after.

As quickly as it began, it's over. One man lies dead in the kitchen and another in the room where Allen and I entered. We begin searching the men, both living and dead. I kneel down over the man's body and find another weapon system. It's a police issue Glock 19. We've been finding these on objectives with greater frequency these days. The pistol is covered in human brains and fragments of the man's skull courtesy of Allen's precision. I put the pistol in a Ziploc bag and place it in my pocket. The spoon is still in the grenade so we carefully replace the pin and add it to a pile of weapons collected throughout the house.

Only once before have I seen a human head look this way. There's no actual structure to the man's skull. His face is still intact for the most part, but it more closely resembles a flaccid mask than a human head. When I was nineteen and working as a firefighter in central Arizona, I was dispatched to a call where a gentlemen was struck by a large pickup truck while walking down the freeway at night. It was the first time I saw a body mangled to such an extent and it stuck with me. Here in this tiny dust-filled bedroom in Iraq I'm transported back to that cold, rainy highway outside of Mayer, Arizona. It's a sight I'm much more capable of coping with this time around, however.

The evening becomes routine at this point. We go through the home looking for any material that can potentially lead us to the next objective. We question some of the young men and women who were in the house, take pictures and package what we think is valuable. By this point I'm thinking if we hurry up we can get back to post in time for midrats. I know I've mentioned midnight rations before, but honestly it really is the best meal of the day. You can get spaghetti and cereal in the same sitting, waffles and steak with a side of eggs and mashed potatoes. Glorious. Years later an ad genius at Taco Bell coined it "Fourth Meal." He musta been a Ranger!

It's common for there to be a shit hole outside of these little mud houses, and this one is no exception. As we make our short foot movement to our exfil point we notice a large hole in the ground several feet deep, filled with human excrement. If you've never walked around in the dark on uneven terrain wearing night vision goggles, it isn't easy. The one's we're using at the time don't provide depth perception, so rolling your ankle in a hole is common. The headquarters element, including the company commander and my good friend Nathan, are the last to make the movement to the exfil point. By the time they're leaving the house our chalk already set a perimeter around where the helos will picking us up. I can see the writing on the wall as the company commander walks out of the target house.

He's easy to identify due to the two large antennas towering over his shoulders from the multiple radios that he carries. I watch in anticipation as he approaches the deep hole full of human shit. Elbowing my Ranger buddy to my right and pointing toward the house, he looks just in time to see the captain disappear into the cavernous fecal abyss. There's a collective attempt at controlling laughter from the entire squad as it appears we're not the only two privileged enough to see the boss take the plunge. With all the strut a Ranger sergeant possesses, my buddy Nathan calmly sidesteps the pitfall and continues to the extraction point. The joke is eventually on us, however. Rather than throwing away the soiled uniform, the CO later decides to wash it communally with the rest of the platoon. For weeks our entire element smells like human waste.

By the time we return and download all of what we've seized and conduct our after action review, the sun is cresting over the desert landscape, and the chow hall is just opening for breakfast. A half dozen of us decide to forego showering immediately for the lure of a hot meal. Outside of the chow hall on most forward operating bases are giant barrels, half buried in the sand with a baseball-sized hole cut in the top of them. They're referred to as clearing barrels and are intended to be used to safely unload your weapon before entering the chow hall. The thing is, most people on a forward operating base never actually have a round in the chamber because they act in a support capacity and seldom, if ever, leave the front gate.

Being a medic, I carry an M9 pistol as well as an M4. This is in the event I have to engage an enemy target while simultaneously working on a wounded individual. It's also highly convenient when traveling around base because it means I don't have to carry a bulky ass rifle.

I feel a tap on my shoulder as I take my first bite of runny scrambled eggs. It's a sergeant from another unit who I don't recognize. He says to me in a nervous voice, "Sergeant, your weapon is condition orange." I have no fucking clue what that means. All I know is that I'm hungry, and when I get hungry, I get hangry. I know we just got done laying hate on a bunch of shithead terrorists. I'm covered in dirt and I still have the remains of that man's brains on my right sleeve. So I reply the only way I know how.

"Cool, bro." I then turn to take a bite of my breakfast. I receive a second tap on the shoulder. The man persists.

"You have a magazine in your weapon, Sergeant."

"You're Goddamn right I do, homeboy. This is Iraq, not Disneyland."

"You can't have a mag in your weapon in the chow hall, Sergeant."

I'm not proud of it, but I lose my cool. I'm not sure if the compounding stress finally gets to me, or I'm just that hungry. I don't maintain my professionalism. I stand up and look that man of equal rank in the eyes, draw my side arm from the holster, drop the mag on the table and clear the round from the chamber. His eyes get fucking huge. The man is just doing his job, but I don't care. He just woke up from a full night's sleep in a comfortable bed.

I feel my right eye tick a little. It's the first time I recall this happening. It still does it to this day in certain situations when I become highly irritated or feel threatened. I ask him if he wouldn't mind leaving me the fuck alone so I can eat my fucking breakfast. He doesn't know what to do. He starts to say something about the clearing barrels outside being the proper something or other. I simply sit down and continue eating. I imagine he just turned and walked away. One of the young privates calmly says, "Jesus, Doc!" and continues with his soggy waffle.

CHAPTER 14

Delirium Trigger

"War is cruelty and you cannot refine it.""
- William Sherman

After several more weeks, the days and nights continue to blur together. I'm not sure what day of the week it is anymore. This is, hands down, the most pain I've ever experienced. I haven't slept in over a week and I think I can officially self-diagnose insomnia. We've been on mission every night for as many nights as I can remember. Everyone in the entire platoon has survived on a constant stream of adrenaline since we landed in Mesopotamia. It's catching up to several of us. I've handed out my entire supply of Ambien to the guys who I feel need it more than I do, so I lay in my bunk staring at the ceiling. It's Iraq in the summer and since we work at night, our down time is midday, and it's fucking hot! Growing up in Phoenix was hot, but Iraq in the summer is fucking hot! As my eyes close and I attempt to find my first moments of sleep there is a tap on my door.

"Hey Doc, sorry to wake you but the compound is flooded."

"What?"

"Yeah, umm I think the Euphrates overflowed or some shit."

"Of course it did. This deployment hasn't been eventful enough, we should add a flood, maybe a plague too."

Our compound is tucked right between where the Euphrates and the Tigris meet. It's surrounded by twenty-foot tall concrete barriers that apparently were not set with any sort of foundation. When the water encompasses them, it erodes the parched dirt beneath, causing them to topple over. As if having helicopters crash, people blowing themselves up, and getting shot at isn't enough, now the walls of our own fortress are trying to kill us! These things have to weigh at least a few tons each, and are toppling over like dominoes all around us. Command makes the decision to move our entire platoon to some tents on the other side of the forward operating base.

I'm not the type who needs any serious degree of luxury. Hell, I've passed out on the floor of a Motel 6 in at least a dozen different states, but these new living conditions fucking suck! They each have a dozen old cots in them and have apparently stood in the desert heat since the initial invasion three years prior. The constant sun exposure has left them literally see-through. It's a hundred and twenty degrees outside the tents and a hundred and thirty inside. This should definitely help the guys get some much-needed sleep! At this point we all we can do is laugh.

"Fuck it! We're all gonna die out here anyway, we can sleep then," jokes one of the team leaders.

The jokes are short-lived. Our platoon sergeant pokes his head into our shitty excuse for living quarters and tells us we just got a mission. I'm borderline delirious during the mission brief. It feels like Groundhog Day and these Red Bull knock-offs have no more effect than a tiny can of water. I can only imagine what drinking ten of these Rip Its a day is doing to my kidneys. *Nephron, cortex, loop of Henle. FOCUS! You're in a mission brief for fuck's sake!*

Okay I'm on chalk two, we're assaulting a target house containing known bomb makers. We go through the motions of jocking up as the sun dissipates like a hunk of butter into the desert frying pan. Our flying chariots touch down in an empty field a few hundred meters from our shitty tent village and we disappear into the night once again.

I don't remember the flight or the infill. The crack of the first shots ringing out on the objective startle me awake. Ah, there's my nightly adrenaline fix! I've got my feet under me now. Me and my boys from second squad chase a couple of guys through a fig orchard. The UH6 Little Bird helicopters are circling above giving us a play-by-play on the direction the two squirters are headed. They start doing gun runs on those poor bastards. There really isn't much you can do when those guns open up; the 160th pilots are the most accurate in the world. They are the reason a lot of special operations guys I know are still on this earth.

For all you would-be terrorists out there, just a heads up, hiding in the dark is easier when you're not wearing a body-length white tunic. We spot one guy laying on the ground to our right. Nick's fire team goes straight for him, pouncing like a pride of lions on a zebra. Joe Gideon and I advance past the commotion toward the second target. His hands are up and both of our rifle barrels are locked on his center mass.

We're both at a full sprint at this point, moving toward him with the knowledge that the violence of action is the only thing that keeps us alive. I know Joe has him covered. Charging like a pair of rhinos, I drop my rifle down to my side by way of the sling and strike the man with such force that he literally goes feet over head, nearly completing a full backflip. The best part is, thanks to the technique I recently learned at the tactical fighting school in Chicago, it didn't hurt my hand one bit. Thanks again, Vanguard!

Joe covers me while I zip tie the man. Meanwhile, one of Nick's guys who's securing the first squirter tells him, "Sergent, my hands are all wet." We avoid using white lights on missions because they have a tendency to make a quick target out of the person holding them. A quick check reveals the gun runs being made by the little bird pilots were effective. The man has a softball size exit wound on his inner left thigh.

The gaping hole makes it tough for him to walk all the way back to the initial target house, but that's his fucking problem. None of our guys are going to carry him. Not after the reports came in from the other squads who cleared the house. They let us know the house these men just fled from is full of bomb-making materials and pictures of high value U.S. targets. No, this shithead gets to walk. You may think that's inhumane, but war is not a movie. Compassion gives way to callousness, and the vegetarian quickly becomes a cannibal.

When we get into the house I'm able to see the extent of his injuries. His scrotum is torn open and his left testicle has completely unraveled as a result of the helicopter raining down hate from the sky. All I can think in the moment is, *holy shit that's a good shot!* The man screams in agony as I stand over him. My glass veins slowly circulate blocks of ice. Empathy? What the fuck is that? I have none at this point. I'm perfectly content to watch this man roll around gripped by the throes of death until we exfil. He has a tourniquet on to stop any major hemorrhage, but I make no effort to pack the wound or help with pain management.

The company commander hears the screams from the other room. He comes in and asks what the situation is. He's former Special Forces so he frequently considers the "hearts and minds" as being an important part of every mission. I'm not going to get into the dynamic of how each faction of special operations works, but I will say that the Green Berets in Special Forces typically have a slightly lighter touch than their Ranger counterparts.

He tells me to administer morphine to the man and pack his wounds. He outranks me by a lot, but not when it comes to patient treatment. On the ground the medic is the authority on all things medical. He's right, though, I can't just leave the guy's nut dangling out, someone might trip over it. I calmly explain to the CO, "I don't carry enough morphine for him and you, so maybe I should hold onto the narcotics I have in case one of our guys gets laced open tonight."

As I kneel down over the man, I'm not sure how to treat an uncoiled testicle. For all of the crazy scenarios drilled into us at SOMC, oddly enough, this one never came up. I decide to use the splayed testicle to help pack the wound in his leg. I can't imagine how it must have felt packing his nut into his open wound with Kerlix then wrapping it with a trauma dressing without any morphine. A testicle when uncoiled is actually quite long. It takes almost a minute to pack the entire thing into his open wound.

Just as I finish up I'm told there's three more squirters in the orchard who we need to secure. We form a small element to track them down. With the air assets we have circling overhead, we figure it'll be a quick game of hide and seek. We trudge through uneven muddy fields for hours taking direction from the guys overhead until we're exhausted. One by one we find all three men and they're not happy when we do, mainly because we're not happy we've gone on a three-hour death march to locate them.

I'm not going to sugarcoat it, I punch one of them in the dick. Hard. Then place my thumb in the wound created by one of our service dogs and use it like a joystick while we look for his other two buddies. This isn't something I'm proud of, but it isn't something I'm ashamed of, either. It's simply the way war is; it's how it makes you and if you haven't been there then you can keep your humanitarian opinion to your damn self. By the time we get back to the cluster of target houses we realize we're not the only ones putting in a hard night's work.

A significant firefight went down in one of the houses. One of the snipers engaged an enemy target through the window of the house. It's an absolutely amazing shot. He's on the rooftop across the street and sees the figure running toward the front door where one of our fire teams is about to make entry, holding a rifle. One shot, straight through the neck. When I examine the person I can tell pretty quickly that, one, it's a woman and two, she's pregnant. When I inform the sniper who made the kill shot of these details it doesn't seem to affect him in the slightest. In fact, he grins the same grin he did in that hangar in Balad when I handed him that atropine injector.

We pile up all of the bomb-making materials and weapons and dispose of them with an incendiary grenade outside in the courtyard. We've gathered a haul of prisoners and information that will likely lead us to the next mission, the next target house filled with people who want us to die. Nearly every night for over three straight months we punch the time card and go to work.

After the mandatory After Action Review (AAR) we head back to our tents. It's ten o'clock in the morning. The desert sun is just starting to seep through the transparent tent ceiling. There isn't even a point to lying down. I escape to the gym in an attempt to burn through this adrenaline. My tiny silk shorts and plain brown t-shirt make me stick out like a sore thumb in the regular Army gym filled with squads of vibrant, well-rested military personnel in their clean grey Army PT uniforms, complete with reflective belt and bad haircut. I get even more dirty looks being the only one doing Olympic lifts and muscle-ups in the corner. It's how I bury all that's transpired. It's another full week and a half-dozen missions before I finally sleep.

They all smear together. The CD skips more aggressively. Creeping through the orchard where Allen engages two sentinels. I get there just after the *zip zip* of shots fired through the suppressor on the end of his M4. The man on the left has a peaceful look on his face, despite his eye dangling near his ear, attached by the optic nerve.

The CD skips and long walks through treacherous streets begging for a fight blur into bedrooms where women cry out for their dead husbands. It's just a thing now. Just a job. It's not noble, or exhilarating, or right or wrong. It's just what it is.

I step around the wrong corner at the wrong time, unaware of the C4 charge on the door to my left. The blast decimates the concrete wall and deforms the steel door frame. First squad flows in as the low purr of white noise dominates my senses. The CD skips. A frag grenade rattles the mud walls of another shack. The CD skips. Allen is wading through waist deep water looking for a squirter. The CD skips. I'm on a knee next to a man with blood pumping from his neck. One of first squad's team leaders shot him. I go through the motions to treat him. I gave more effort to the goats back in school. This pile of quivering meat before me is no longer a human. Just an opportunity to practice my skills. It wasn't always this way. The CD skips.

One of my final missions as a Ranger is in June of 2006. Like so many of the nights before we're tasked with finding, and if need be, eliminating a high value target. We land in a small valley about a kilometer from the target house. It's a straight sprint up. About half way up I feel an aggressive pop in my abdomen. My right leg becomes heavy all of a sudden. I'm not entirely sure in the moment, but I suspect my abdominal wall just ruptured. Slowing down isn't an option though. We make it to the front door of the target house and clear through with the precision of an experienced surgeon.

We don't even talk to each other at this point in the deployment as we move seamlessly through the dark house. We clear every single room and find ourselves on the rooftop where about a dozen women and children were sleeping. This is common in Iraq in the summer months, as it's typically cooler on the roof than inside the house.

The ground floor is secure. It appears as though we just hit a dry hole. After conducting a back search, the all clear is given. We begin conducting a search for sensitive materials and weapons. I'm in a room by myself looking through a series of dresser drawers. I find a significant amount of material on bomb making as well as documents connecting the homeowner with Saddam Hussein. After all of the drawers are tossed, I focus my attention on a basket of clothes near the window. I kneel down to sift through the soiled white tunics. Just as I do, my left ear picks up an odd sound. It's a buzzing I'm familiar with, but haven't heard in a while. I look left, but it's too late. The buzzing is gone. I go back to sifting. Ten seconds later I hear the noise again. This time, I immediately look left and see a glow just above my head. *FUCK! That's a cell phone!*

That's a cell phone in someone's pocket!

That's a cell phone in a terrorist's pocket, in a hidden location, less than a foot away from me!

I'm on my feet in a fraction of a second, weapon orientated on target, safety off, finger on the trigger! But I don't squeeze.

I call for the guy in the other room. He's beside me in an instant. I tell him the situation, and both of our rifles raise and fixate on the corner. We can't see the man because he's hidden well behind a closet door. "Doc, we should shoot this guy," I hear whispered from the man to my left. As the final word passes his lips, the door moves violently. I let a volley of eight shots loose on his position.

The man's limp body falls through his hiding position and onto the dusty floor. A call comes over the radio to determine where the shots came from. My superior officer asks, "Who's shooting?"

"Umm, it was me," is all my rattled voice can muster.

Since there's about forty of us all connected on the same channel, this is not an appropriate response. Like the veteran platoon sergeant he is, SFC Strait sends it with salt, "Yeah, and who are you, asshole?"

I break another cardinal rule by saying my name rather than my call sign (a number or nickname assigned to help soldiers maintain anonymity). I give my location and within seconds a good friend of mine enters the room and gives the lifeless man two more shots to the head for the sake of being fastidious.

I'm almost positive I'm going to prison for what I just did. My entire life society has taught me not to kill and when you do there are severe consequences. To my surprise, one of my superiors walks in and gives me a high five, and like that it's over. I tell my story and everyone seems excited. I don't understand. Later I find out the man I shot is one of the primary high value targets in Iraq. He's a "bad guy," a really bad guy, by our definition. So why should I feel bad? I eliminated a villain.

Here's the crux. I receive a medal announcing to the world I'm a hero for eliminating a threat to our nation. In reality, I become a murderer while giving this man martyrdom. Or did I have it right the first time? I guess if you ask my family they'd say I'm the hero, if you ask his family they'd say he is. Then again, my family hasn't heard the full story, but neither has his. They likely don't know he's responsible for the death of hundreds of people. That he used that same cell phone to detonate roadside bombs. Or is that how I justify my actions to be able to sleep at night? Does it matter? I don't have the answer to that. All I know is as I sit here typing, that God-forsaken award hangs from the wall over my right shoulder. And if I did not covet honor so much I would burn it like the piece of hypocritical trash it is.

Returning from another all-night mission.

Flying over the Euphrates. Summer of 2006.

CHAPTER 15

The Broken

"I must study politics and war that my sons may have liberty to study
mathematics and philosophy."
- John Adams

The following evening, we roll out the gates again. This time in a convoy of eight-wheel vehicles called Strykers. They're somewhere between a tank and a troop carrier. We sit shoulder-to-shoulder, packed like sardines in the back, rumbling down the bombed-out streets. Every bump an excruciating reminder of the injury to my abdominal wall. The plates in my body armor are exacerbating my discomfort. I must be wearing that pain on my face; SFC Strait comments about how green I look. I'm trying so hard to man up, but I must be failing. It feels like I'm simultaneously being stabbed in the groin and punched in the stomach. It's at least one hundred and ten degrees in this hot metal box. All of my attention is focused firmly on not vomiting.

We make it through the mission without incident. When we return to base the Battalion PA confirms my suspicion. My abdominal injury has made me combat ineffective. He suggests surgery back in the U.S. We only have a couple more weeks of this deployment. I didn't think he would suggest I go home.

A couple of days later I'm sent back to the States to have surgery. My platoon stays in harm's way for three more weeks. They engage in more violence, more chaos, while I'm safe. They have another crack at Abu Musab al-Zarqawi and experience the calamity of a Little Bird crash. As much discomfort as I'm in, nothing hurts worse than not being there for my guys. It's the worst kind of pain. I barely sleep for the next three weeks waiting for them to return. I drink literally every day, and not in a celebratory fashion. Knowing my family is still there without me is a torment unlike anything that I've ever experienced. I drown myself in opaque oceans, poured a pint at a time. I'm relieved to be home, but hate myself for telling anyone about my injury.

When my platoon returns, we celebrate in true Ranger fashion. No one speaks of the countless near-death experiences or people's lives we took. We raise and drain our glasses, then move on. One of my mentors is getting out of the army right after they got home. I've never been good with goodbyes. I'm no stranger to them at this point. A lot of guys come in and out of your life in the military. It's not that you don't love them, it's just important to understand anyone can go at any time. Understanding this makes it much easier to detach and compartmentalize when someone is taken out of your life abruptly. Dave is a little different though. We worked together so closely as platoon medics for years. Dave taught me a lot of the little things that make a great medic. He'd been a role model for me when I first got to battalion. His leaving is like having a big brother move away from home. I try to avoid most of the celebration by staying at home, but receive a dozen texts asking, "Where the fuck are you, Doc?"

A little drunk doesn't begin to describe the condition Dave is in by the time I arrive. There's a handful of guys from our company who I recognize as I enter the bar. Dave is slouched over at his bar stool with his forehead resting on his left forearm.

"What's up, buddy?"

Dave peels his head off the bar and attempts to focus on me. The movement is far more laborious than it should be. He bobbles around for a bit before falling back on his forearm. I look back at my good friend, Nathan. "He's not looking so good."

"Oh, Dave's fucked up!" Nathan says with a laugh.

Nathan is a burly Viking of a man. He has hands like hammers and stands over six feet tall.

I start to ask Nathan how long they've been here when I hear the violent splatter of Dave throwing up on the floor.

"Ahhh shit, Dave just puked. We're totally getting kicked out of here," Nathan says while laughing. Dave wipes the vomit from his mouth with his sleeve while picking his head up to see if anyone noticed. He plays it off with a move I don't expect. He gets the attention of the bartender and orders another shot. The stones on this guy. There's no way in hell the bartender is going to . . . and he's pouring Dave another shot! What the fuck? He shoots the Jager like a five-meter target. Just as I start to comment about Dave being a champ, he puts his head in his other arm and throws up down his other pant leg.

"Maybe we should go," Nathan chimes in again.

"Yeah, that's probably not a bad idea," I respond.

We pay Dave's bar tab and help him out the door. Most of the other guys relocated to a bar across the street so it's just Nathan, Dave, Flippy, and me. Flippy is our company's training room NCO. He's a good guy, not the biggest guy, but a Ranger through and through. Needless to say, Dave isn't walking too straight. There's a lot of construction going on in downtown Columbus. There's an eight-foot-tall, chain link fence that runs the length of the curb, creating a corridor. The sidewalk is about ten feet wide and there's a row of bars and shops to our left, the chain link fence to our right. Nathan and I walk behind Dave, laughing as he repeatedly stumbles into the huge windows of the store fronts.

"Hey! Asshole, knock it off!" shouts some random guy standing outside of Scruffy Murphy's Irish Pub. So of course Dave now intentionally slams himself into the next large window, pissing off the random guy further. He starts speed walking toward Dave. I know that in his condition there's no way Dave will be able to defend himself. As the guy gets within a few feet of my Ranger buddy, I hockey check him into the wall. It catches him off guard; he may not have realized that Nathan and I are friends with the guy he's trying to pick a fight with. In true tough-guy fashion, he puts his hands up, completely exposing himself, and exclaims, "Bitch, you don't know me!"

I calmly respond, "Well, you don't know me," as I punch him in the mouth, uncomfortably stretching the seams of my recently healed incision. In all the MMA bouts, combat missions, and tactical fighting schools I've been through, I have never hit someone with such force. His knees buckle and he drops like a limp sack of shit.

As he hits the ground I hear the thump-sting ring out in my ear. It's the sound of getting punched in the side of the head. *What the fuck? Where did that come from?* As I turn and face whoever struck me, someone else pulls my shirt up over my head hockey style. *Where the fuck did he come from?* Now I'm getting punched from two different people and I can't even see who they are. I'm swinging wildly to try to create some distance. I manage to get my shirt off completely. A quick assessment of the situation reveals that Flippy is flat on his back getting his face stomped by a couple of guys. It looks like we kicked a hornet's nest. There's eight of them. *Where the fuck did they all come from?* I look to my left just in time to see Nathan one punch some guy in the face. As the guy is collapsing, Nathan turns and services another target, and another. I'm in absolute awe. He just knocked out three guys in a matter of seconds. I look to my right and see Dave has a hold of that chain link fence. He is kneeing the shit out of it Muay Thai style screaming, "Fuck you, bitch!" Dave just started this whole thing and his drunken ass is fighting the chain link fence. Classic.

I knock one of the guys off Flippy, giving him enough space to get up. I start backing up preparing for one of these idiots to pull out a weapon. As I'm backing up I bump into someone. I turn to face him, fists up, ready to strike. To my surprise he's in uniform. He has on a beautiful tan beret. "You Rangers?" he asks.

"Roger."

"I'm staff duty, come on let's get the fuck out of here."

Nathan and Flip grab Dave and we back away. The three guys still on their feet try to help their five buddies up, and don't attempt to chase us. The staff duty truck is across the street. Just as we're getting in, we see those damn red and blue lights. *SHIT!* As the cop steps out of his squad car, I see two girls walking down the street. I change direction and begin walking with them acting like I don't know those other guys. It almost works, too. Almost. The officer hollers at me and I respond, "I don't know those guys." Like most things, I attempt to turn it into a big joke. He collects all of our IDs. *Well, looks like we're going to jail.* Just as he has all of our licenses, some random guy in a muscle car pulls up and yells, "FUCK YOU!" to the cop and peels out.

The officer hands our IDs to the staff duty NCO and tells us, "Wait here," as he gets into his car to chase that beautiful drunk asshole who just burnt rubber.

"So you guys want to wait around for that cop to come back and arrest us?"

"Fuck that!"

"Good call, Nathan!"

The staff duty NCO takes us all home, one by one.

The next morning when we arrive at Battalion, Flip has a boot print tattooed on his face. Dave and Nathan are hungover beyond belief. I still can't believe Dave took that shot of Jager after throwing up. After our morning formation, Nathan decides he's going to go home. It's not the first time he cut out of work eleven hours early.

Nathan isn't around when we get called into the First Sergeant's office. First Sergeant Sealy, "The Rhino," was with our platoon for most of our missions in Iraq. I've never seen a more physically imposing human on the field of battle. The man's legs are thicker than my waist. He's built like an NFL linebacker with close to twenty years as a Ranger. He's one of the only First Sergeants I've ever known to have a beer with the privates in his company. He knows the strength of the Regiment is the men and is consistently willing to listen to their opinions. On this day, however, he arrived to work and received a phone call from staff duty informing him that some of the guys in his company were in a drunken brawl the night before. That put him in a bad mood.

I'm running sick call in my aid station when Flip comes in and tells me the 1SG is pissed and we have thirty seconds to get into his office. The ass chewing which follows can be heard by the guys in the chow hall. He. Is.

Pissed. He yells at us, "When staff duty told me that some of my Rangers got in a fight downtown while we're on IRC, I thought I was going to have to kick four privates out of Ranger Battalion. Then I find out it is my senior company medic, training room NCO, and commo chief. Wait, where the fuck is Nathan? You assholes know if you'd been arrested you would have fucked the entire company? What the fuck were you thinking you dumb—"

I interrupt, "First Sergeant . . "

I realize now the question he's asking is strictly rhetorical, and he didn't really want any of us to say a damn thing. His eyes get even bigger as he focuses them directly at my soul.

"First Sergeant, we were only doing what we were trained to do, we were looking after another Ranger."

He takes a deep breath in. He wants to destroy me right now, but I can see in his eyes, he knows our intention. "GET THE FUCK OUT!!" he yells.

We don't hesitate. The three of us scurry for the door the way a dog does when it's been kicked in the ass for shitting on the rug. We get back to the aid station and call Nathan; he doesn't answer. He's probably sleeping. What a shithead. At least he doesn't have to walk around the rest of the day with a boot print on his face.

Less than a month later, it's my turn close this chapter in my life. Like my first return from overseas, there's no ceremony. Everyone is busy preparing for another training event. There's no going-away party when my time comes, no plaque, no farewell. My platoon sergeant, a man who I once feared and now have an infinite respect for, jokes that I'm always getting over when there's work to be done. I tell him it's been an honor being his medic and shake his hand. I walk back into my aid station for the last time to hang my dog tags from the ceiling alongside each of the medics who've come and gone before me. I walk out the door without anyone noticing. The drive out of the brown fence begins my tumultuous assimilation back to civility and the world after war.

In four short years, I drank a beer in forty-six states. I conducted a hundred real-world missions as a Special Operations Medic, some good, some bad, every one a learning experience. I helped some men to live, while taking the lives of others. I was trusted with the health and well-being of our nation's heroes. I learned more about myself in a couple of years than most men will in a lifetime. I lost friends and gained scars. The confidence I take away from this experience is, to this day, my most valuable character trait; it is also what alienates me from most people.

Above all else, I worked side-by-side with the best men of our generation. Men who would have no doubt fought beside Leonidas at Thermopylae had they been born 2,500 years sooner. These men are the greatest hope of our generation. They are altruism, they are benevolence. They are terror in the hearts of the enemy. They are blue collar farmers and college graduates, doctors and business owners. They are fathers, brothers, and sons. They have carried the burden of our nation. They are my friends . . . my brothers . . . and forever will be.

Lest We Forget their contribution.

More works by Leo Jenkins...

On Assimilation: A Ranger's Return from War

Some wars don't end, some scars don't heal, and some bonds can't be broken. Former U.S. Army Ranger Medic, Leo Jenkins, picks up where he left off with his best-selling book, Lest We Forget to explore the tribulations associated with attempting to reintegrate back into society after years at war. In what is being considered one of the most significant introspective on veteran transition issues ever written, Jenkins lays it all on the line one more time with On Assimilation, A Ranger's Return from War.

An Excerpt:

As Christmas approached, we made contact with a reserve unit stationed at a small forward operating base (FOB) about five miles away. The post commander graciously invited us to have Christmas dinner with his unit, an invitation that we were most grateful for. The men that cooked in our tiny chow hall worked very hard for us, but there is something very necessary about a larger gathering during these times. This was not my first Christmas in Afghanistan and to say that I missed my family was an understatement.

On the short drive to the Army FOB, I allowed my mind to wander to my father's back porch where my siblings, nieces, and nephews had inevitably gathered to share each other's company. There would no doubt be a couple of bottles of whiskey sitting out, all of my siblings' children were running and playing with their new toys, while all of the adults sat around the table and told stories and joked as the sun settled over the desert mountain range, causing the sky to explode with a vibrant myriad of color and life.

Instantly, I was transported back to the tenebrous frigid reality of my current isolation as we approach the gate of the FOB. My heart was filled with gratitude as we were welcomed into the plywood dining hall. I had not realized it until then, but the look on my face was different than these soldiers. Although it had only been a couple of years since I wore the same uniform, I felt as though I had aged well beyond them. Their eyes did not seem at all heavy. I could somehow feel the weight of all the killing and surviving hanging from my face, my thick beard doing little to conceal its burden.

I thought back to twenty-two years old, sitting at a very similar table. As I took my seat, a slideshow of years at war, both overseas and with myself, rapidly flashed before me. I can see now that the tribulations endured during those fateful nights in Iraq while bringing violence to the den of the wolf paled in comparison to the affliction of parting ways with those who shared that experience. In that moment, I knew that the worst of war that these men would ever endure would be that of leaving it behind.

First Train Out of Denver

Leo has a decision to make—maintain a comfortable position in a career he's no longer passionate about—or take a massive leap of faith. Equal parts social philosophy and travel adventure, First Train Out of Denver takes the reader on an around the world quest for meaning in a seamlessly senseless world. Along the way, Leo accepts a challenge from another former Army Ranger to see how far they can travel together in three weeks with nothing but a backpack and one hundred dollars to raise awareness and funds for a veteran charity. By any means necessary, the two manage to traverse two continents and film an award-winning documentary along the way.

An Excerpt:

The places to go and sights to see on this continent are as near infinite as the stars above it. Perhaps that's why I feel so tiny, so alone. Marty and I created an effective pattern of quickly saying goodbye to each passing host, yet always maintaining one another's company. In a similar fashion, when it was time for him to return to the States, he pressed on as though still on our mission. I did the same, just in the opposite direction. A stoic separation appropriate for two aging soldiers, neither investing emotional coin on departing from a good friend. Even after all we accomplished, we overcame, and grew with one another, the most fitting farewell confined to, *I'll see you when I see you.*

Now for the first time, I am completely unaccompanied and attempting to digest the magnitude of all that has transpired. I've never experienced a more painful solitude amidst such a dense population. A grey haze blankets even the most luminous human experience when traversed alone.

I spend my final night in Europe watching the U.S. lose another World Cup match, surrounded by different groups of tourist travelers in the city of

Prague. The long walk back to my hotel room is protracted by my lack of bearing. I'm lost.

Alone. Adrift. Among a sea of faces and cackling conversations. Searching for a road that leads home. Seeking solace in familiarity but finding none. The agony of this evolution continues. Departure from comfort is simply the seed. Transcendence into a towering oak of internal faith begins with that seed. What great man has ever been, who was not first self-reliant? What person ever came to that state without first experiencing the anguish of isolation?

Coming soon…

Disarming Tragedy: The Mary Dague Interview

Leo Jenkins sits down with US Army EOD Technician, Mary Dague, to discuss her experience being critically injured in Iraq, the process of healing, and returning home. One of the most inspiring stories of the Global War on Terrorism, told by one of its most humble participants. Mary holds nothing back in this one of a kind memoir interview. Mary and Leo go shot for shot on war stories and whiskey alike in one of the most raw, real war stories to date.

Suggested reading…

Violence of Action:
The Untold Stories of the 75th Ranger Regiment in the War on Terror

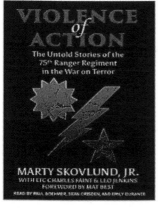

Violence of Action is much more than the true, first-person accounts of the 75th Ranger Regiment in the Global War on Terror. Between these pages are the heartfelt, first-hand accounts from, and about, the men who lived, fought, and died for their country, their Regiment, and each other. Objective Rhino, Haditha Dam, recovering Jessica Lynch, the hunt for Zarqawi, the recovery of Extortion 17 and everything in between… These stories have been told many times in barracks rooms, bar tables, and backyard barbecues but they have never before been shared with the general public. It is time for those stories to be heard.

So much more than just stories from a specific unit; this book reveals the sights, smells, and emotions of everything that happens in war - good or bad. It will be seen as the quintessential, ageless work on the human condition in combat. Whether you served in the military, are a fan of military history, or just want to know more about your fellow man in times of war - this is the book for you.

The Ghosts of Babylon
(Foreword by Leo Jenkins)

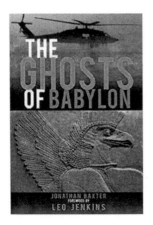

The Ghosts of Babylon offers eyewitness accounts of warriors who lost their innocence dueling in the sands of the Iraqi inferno or fighting in the chilling Afghan mountains or on the khaki-colored plains. Wounds enshrouded under the bandages of headlines and sound bites will never bridge the gap between soldier and civilian.

Only a soldier poet lays bare the honor and horror. Only a veteran reveals the physical and mental battles waged by the warrior caste. Only the war poet distills the emotions of those who tasted bravery and terror, love and vengeance, life and death. Based on the experiences of a U.S. Army Ranger turned private security contractor, these powerful poems capture the essence of Jonathan Baxter's twelve military and civilian deployments.

Jonathan reveals the contradictory nature of deployment in a war zone— exhilaration, monotony, ugliness, and occasional beauty. From ancient times to present day, war poetry telegraphs a dispatch across the ages about the universal experiences of war—brotherhood and bereavement, duty and disillusionment, and heroism and horror. No history mirrors the brutal realities and emotions of armed conflict than the shock of war erupting from the warrior poet's pen.

73544924R00099

Made in the USA
Middletown, DE
15 May 2018